NAPA VALLEY

NAPA VALLEY

The Ultimate Winery Guide

REVISED AND UPDATED, FOURTH EDITION

By Antonia Allegra

Photographs by Richard Gillette

Foreword by Robert Mondavi

CHRONICLE BOOKS

SAN FRANCISCO

Library of Congress Cataloging-in-Publication Data available.

ISBN 0-8118-4088-3

Manufactured in Singapore.

Book design and cover by Susan Park

Distributed in Canada by Raincoast Books
9050 Shaughnessy Street
Vancouver, British Columbia V6P 6E5

10 9 8 7 6 5 4 3 2 1

Chronicle Books LLC
85 Second Street
San Francisco, California 94105

www.chroniclebooks.com

DEDICATION

For Donn, John, Jane, Deanna, Paul, Sue, Orion, Kathy, Madeline, Alex, Jenny, Marty, Ethan, Alex B., and all my family and friends who gather at the Treehouse.

—Antonia

For my daughters Jasara and Holly and grandchildren Zachary Martín and Natalie Lynn, Sandra McMahon, Dan and Bonnie Borghi, Shanti Finnerty, Chuck and Camille Hathaway, and the rest of my Mendocino family.

—Richard

Without their inspiration, support, laughter, and love, this book would not exist.

ACKNOWLEDGMENTS

We extend special thanks to these people who went out of their way to help us create this book, in each of its editions: Maynard Amerine, Maria Lorraine Binchet, Sara Bir, Michael Carabetta, Martha Casselman, Carey Charlesworth, Jodi Davis, Mary Frances Kennedy Fisher, Jim Frisinger, Phil Hiaring, Kelly Johnson, Leslie Jonath, Bill LeBlond, Lisa Levin, Harvey Posert, Stephanie Rosenbaum, Ellen Russell, Bill Ryan, Bob Steinhauer, and John and Gladys Wichels.

CONTENTS

FOREWORD

Welcome to our lovely Napa Valley and to all its wineries! Whether you journey on Highway 29 or the Silverado Trail or take the armchair route through the pages of this book, you'll find numerous older wineries and many new ones eager to show you our renowned hospitality. Through the winery tours and your visits in our towns and restaurants, your enjoyment of wine will grow as you learn more about this land and its wonderful people. ⌘ Each winery has its own point of view about grape growing and wine making—that's what makes wine so interesting. As you visit the individual wineries, ask about special programs on wine making, on the arts, and on wine and food. We all want to play a part in forming your happy memories of this valley. ⌘ Bringing wine together with the arts and culture has been a special focus of my career. Even though ours is one of the newer wineries—it was one of the first wineries built after Prohibition, in 1966—we join in a long tradition of wine and gastronomy as well as the fine arts: music, painting, sculpture, theater, writing, and, here especially, architecture. ⌘ Wine is the natural beverage for every celebration: the birth of a child, graduation, engagements, weddings, anniversaries, promotions, family gatherings, toasts between governments, and many other occasions. Wine can stand the scrutiny of any responsible citizen because its benefits have been recognized for more than seven thousand years . . . since civilization began. And common sense tells us that wine will be with us forever as an integral part of our culture, heritage, and gracious way of life. ⌘ I always knew that Napa Valley had the soils, climate, grape varieties, and people to make wines that rank on a par with the finest wines of the world. Fortunately, in the past decades we have been able to show connoisseurs in the Old and New Worlds that this is so; and we hope that you will share our enthusiasm, success, and enjoyment.

I raise a glass to the many guests who will enjoy this book and to their visits in the Napa Valley.

"To your health!"

Robert Mondavi
Oakville, California

AN
INVITATION

INTRODUCTION

The play of color against the thirty-mile symmetry of neat vineyards bonds visitors and residents to Napa Valley. As you drive along the two north-south thoroughfares, the gentle mountain ranges act as backdrop to spectacular views, dappled with vineyard colors that depend on the time of year—the bright yellow of mustard plants at the feet of dormant vines in spring; a rich, verdant carpet of summer's grape leaves; the autumn olive, rust, burgundy, and sienna of a Renaissance tapestry; and, finally, the somber black and brown tones of winter. Sometimes, seen from an auto at fifty miles per hour, trellis wires give the impression of sheets of silver. The quality of light in this region is often extraordinary and has been the inspiration for many an artist's eye. If your eye grabs a point and moves with it, you will see a blur of color. But allow the view to skip from row to row of vines and it will seem to be a series of mirrors, channels reflecting plants in various stages of life. In fact, it is the constant awareness of the life-growth-harvest cycle of renewal that invokes reflectiveness throughout the year. The Napa Valley has been an agricultural hub since well before the Civil War. This was originally home to the Wappo and other tribes of Native Americans. Then, under General Mariano Vallejo, the area became Mexican California until the Bear Flag Republic revolt. In those early years, wheat, apples, prunes, walnuts, and a few grapevines were planted in the rocky soil. With the Victorian boom and the rise in popularity of locally made wines, the region flourished socially as well as agriculturally. The Prohibition years (1919–1933) closed most wineries and halted local development, but the valley has thrived since the mid-1960s and is again a popular visitors' spot. It has been named the third most popular natural tourist attraction in the state of California, following San Francisco and Yosemite. Napa, Yountville, Oakville, Rutherford, St. Helena, and Calistoga dot the thirty-mile-long, five-mile-wide string of towns and cities along Highway 29 and the Silverado Trail. They act as centers for the locals and lodging, dining, and shopping places for visitors. But most of the valley's activity happens in the fields. ☙ Ninety percent of this valley is dedicated to agricultural use, and, unlike neighboring Sonoma County, most of the earth on this side of the Mayacamas Range is planted to vines. Hillsides and meadows of cattle, horses, sheep, or goats are rare here. At an average of one hundred fifty thousand to two hundred thousand dollars a "valley floor acre" planted to Cabernet or Chardonnay, the land is too expensive for any cultivation other than grapes. As a result, this is an American wine-lover's paradise. ☙ Those who have visited the wine regions of Europe will see similarities in the rocky grape-growing terrains and occasionally in the vistas. However, I believe that there is one major difference from the tourist's point of view: in Europe, a vineyard visit is just that, a walk in the vineyard, if you're lucky. More often, it is a descent into a cool basement to taste some wine and make a purchase. If you wish to see imposing architecture accessible to the public, you must travel to the various chateaux regions that often are near but separated from the vineyards. And they often require special reservations. ☙ Here in the Napa Valley, a visitor has the best of all worlds. Superb wines are available at any of more than 400 wineries, and often the establishments are housed in magnificent structures themselves worthy of castle visits. As it turns out, winery owners are the royalty of the Napa Valley, their kingdoms being vineyards and wineries. ☙ Perhaps this valley is so loved because it offers a magical sense of familiarity. For instance, this could easily be the setting for Jack and the Beanstalk's Happy Valley of fairy-tale lore. And millions viewed these hills and vineyards weekly during the screening of the *Falcon Crest* television series. But even more, being here feels like a homecoming to the best of rural America's simple life. ☙ In my hometown of St. Helena, certain daily observations still strike me as gifts rather than facts of life. I have lived in big cities, and nothing there offers such basic pleasure as the morning greeting from the postman when I pick up my mail or the sound of frogs croaking on starry spring nights. The OK Barber Shop on Main Street hasn't changed its interior in more than fifty years, and its dull-green, ecru, and chrome fixtures aren't likely to switch to those of a styling salon. Crusty country loaves continue to exit hot from the Model Baker's brick oven, and the town merchants chatter in the morning light as they sweep their sidewalk footage. And a call-to-alarm alerts volunteer fire department members and townspeople of some strain in the otherwise calm life of the town. ☙ There are other images, too. There's a freckled boy—maybe ten years old—who frequently bicycles to school, tugging his laughing pal on a skateboard tied to the end of a rope. There is a sweet down-home honesty about this place. ☙ Ever-present birds add their joyful touch to daily life. Occasionally a flock of red-winged blackbirds swoops to a fence rail, exposing a sudden surprise of

brilliant red feathers at their shoulders. Or, when unpicked grapes still hang like udders from vines in December, it's not unusual for the sky to be filled with careening, twittering starlings, drunk from the yeasty vineyard fruit. ℰ Many Napa Valley residents grow grapes instead of lawns. With the drought of the 1980s and 1990s, a vineyard became more practical, requiring no mowing and yielding wine grapes that could be sold or pressed into wine. In fact, the residents can "drink their lawns." ℰ Where else in America would you see a "No Winery This Lane" sign along the highway? Or find almost three pages of winery listings in the telephone book? ℰ Often, with nearly four hundred wineries on a valley list, it can be difficult to choose which to visit. And friends have told me, "We can't go wrong tasting Napa Valley wines, but we want to visit Victorian homes, too." To guide their preferences, I developed a personal annotated list for family and friends. Wineries with art collections. Spectacular gardens. Technical tours. Once on a serious path, I toured and screened wineries in the valley that are open to visitors. The wineries had to offer tours and be easily accessible, interesting, and visitor-friendly. To write this book, I finally identified the twenty-eight wineries that I believe fascinate and entertain visitors most with their Napa Valley wine-making art and way of life. My list is by no means meant to limit you in your travels in the Napa Valley. All the wineries here are marvelous, each with a different story

and beauty. These are the wineries I suggest to my friends. ✑ In all cases, I took standard tours. I did not seek or accept any gifts. The wineries chosen are here because they go out of their way to make visiting an educational and sensual pleasure. For this fourth edition of the guide, I visited all wineries on these pages here as well as many others to make the final choices for your touring pleasure. Since the 2000 edition, I have found profound upgrading of facilities, tours, and shops throughout the valley. ✑ I do not wish to overlook the multiple ways to view the Napa Valley. By air, there are hot air balloons, gliders, and biplanes. You can travel by bicycle or horse or train, or you can hike. And the possibilities for outstanding meals here are legendary. ✑ No matter how you visit our valley, no matter whether you stay at a resort, a hotel, a bed and breakfast inn, or in your friend's guest room, expect daily brushes with beauty mixed with the reality of the vineyard year. The combination may catch you unaware. Though this splendid valley of vines and winery "castles" may seem small, its greatness will be evident—in its people and in its wines.

Antonia Allegra
St. Helena, California

OVERVIEW

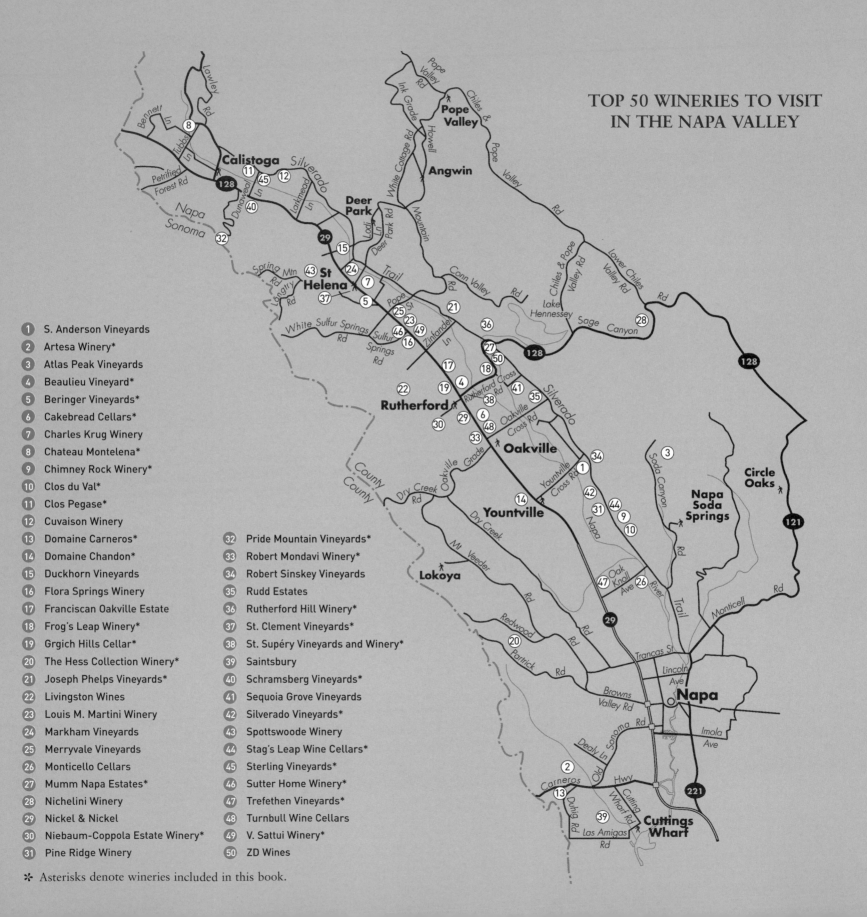

TOP 50 WINERIES TO VISIT
IN THE NAPA VALLEY

1 S. Anderson Vineyards
2 Artesa Winery*
3 Atlas Peak Vineyards
4 Beaulieu Vineyard*
5 Beringer Vineyards*
6 Cakebread Cellars*
7 Charles Krug Winery
8 Chateau Montelena*
9 Chimney Rock Winery*
10 Clos du Val*
11 Clos Pegase*
12 Cuvaison Winery
13 Domaine Carneros*
14 Domaine Chandon*
15 Duckhorn Vineyards
16 Flora Springs Winery
17 Franciscan Oakville Estate
18 Frog's Leap Winery*
19 Grgich Hills Cellar*
20 The Hess Collection Winery*
21 Joseph Phelps Vineyards*
22 Livingston Wines
23 Louis M. Martini Winery
24 Markham Vineyards
25 Merryvale Vineyards
26 Monticello Cellars
27 Mumm Napa Estates*
28 Nichelini Winery
29 Nickel & Nickel
30 Niebaum-Coppola Estate Winery*
31 Pine Ridge Winery

32 Pride Mountain Vineyards*
33 Robert Mondavi Winery*
34 Robert Sinskey Vineyards
35 Rudd Estates
36 Rutherford Hill Winery*
37 St. Clement Vineyards*
38 St. Supéry Vineyards and Winery*
39 Saintsbury
40 Schramsberg Vineyards*
41 Sequoia Grove Vineyards
42 Silverado Vineyards*
43 Spottswoode Winery
44 Stag's Leap Wine Cellars*
45 Sterling Vineyards*
46 Sutter Home Winery*
47 Trefethen Vineyards*
48 Turnbull Wine Cellars
49 V. Sattui Winery*
50 ZD Wines

✽ Asterisks denote wineries included in this book.

THE OPERATIONS OF A VINEYARD YEAR

JANUARY: Weeding, spraying, pruning, vine tying/vine training, major machinery maintenance

FEBRUARY: Pruning, vine tying/vine training, major machinery maintenance, rootstock pulled from nursery/stored, budwood selection/storage

MARCH: Vine tying/vine training, cultivating/discing, frost control

APRIL: Planting rootstock and benchgrafts, cultivating/discing, foliar spraying–fertilization, irrigation, frost control, suckering (removing undesirable shoots), sulfuring (to prevent mildew), fertilizing, vine tying/vine training

MAY: Irrigation, foliar spraying on leaves, planting, suckering, cultivating/discing, frost control, fertilizing, vine tying/vine training, sulfuring

JUNE: Foliar spraying on leaves, cultivating/discing, suckering, grafting, irrigation, frost control, crop thinning, fertilizing, vine tying/vine training, sulfuring

JULY: Cultivating/discing, irrigation, vine tying/vine training, berry (actual description of and industry name for grape) sampling

AUGUST: Irrigation, hedging, harvesting, grafting, berry sampling, ongoing installation of irrigation and frost control systems, vineyard development operations, soil preparation

SEPTEMBER: Harvesting, grafting, berry sampling, ongoing installation of irrigation and frost control systems, vineyard development operations, soil preparation

OCTOBER: Harvesting, ongoing installation of irrigation and frost control systems, vineyard development operations, soil preparation

NOVEMBER: Major machinery maintenance, weed spraying, chiseling (breaking up soil compaction), ongoing installation of irrigation and frost control systems, vineyard development operations, soil preparation

DECEMBER: Major machinery maintenance, weed spraying, ongoing installation of irrigation and frost control systems, vineyard development operations, soil preparation

WINERY TOURS

WINERY TOURS

WINERIES BY NAPA VALLEY REGION

DOWN-VALLEY (SOUTH)
Artesa Winery
Chimney Rock Winery
Clos du Val
Domaine Carneros
Domaine Chandon
The Hess Collection Winery
Stag's Leap Wine Cellars
Trefethen Vineyards

MID-VALLEY (CENTRAL)
Beaulieu Vineyard
Cakebread Cellars
Grgich Hills Cellar
Robert Mondavi Winery
Mumm Napa Estates
Niebaum-Coppola Estate Winery
Rutherford Hill Winery
St. Supéry Vineyards and Winery
Silverado Vineyards

UP-VALLEY (NORTH)
Beringer Vineyards
Chateau Montelena
Clos Pegase
Frog's Leap Winery
Joseph Phelps Vineyards
Pride Mountain Vineyards
St. Clement Vineyards

Schramsberg Vineyards
Sterling Vineyards
Sutter Home Winery
V. Sattui Winery

WINERIES BY TOWN

CALISTOGA
Chateau Montelena
Clos Pegase
Schramsberg Vineyards
Sterling Vineyards

NAPA
Artesa Winery
Chimney Rock Winery
Clos du Val
Domaine Carneros
The Hess Collection Winery
Silverado Vineyards
Stag's Leap Wine Cellars
Trefethen Vineyards

OAKVILLE
Robert Mondavi Winery

RUTHERFORD
Beaulieu Vineyard
Cakebread Cellars
Frog's Leap Winery
Grgich Hills Cellar
Mumm Napa Estates

Niebaum-Coppola Estate Winery
Rutherford Hill Winery
St. Supéry Vineyards and Winery

ST. HELENA
Beringer Vineyards
Joseph Phelps Vineyards
Pride Mountain Vineyards
St. Clement Vineyards
Sutter Home Winery
V. Sattui Winery

YOUNTVILLE
Domaine Chandon

IDEAL VISITING SEASONS FOR WINERIES

WINTER
Chimney Rock Winery
Domaine Carneros
The Hess Collection Winery
Pride Mountain Vineyards

SPRING
Artesa Winery
Beringer Vineyards
Domaine Chandon
Frog's Leap Winery
Niebaum-Coppola Estate Winery
Joseph Phelps Vineyards
Sterling Vineyards

SUMMER
Chateau Montelena
Clos Pegase
Grgich Hills Cellar
Rutherford Hill Winery
Schramsberg Vineyards
Silverado Vineyards
Stag's Leap Wine Cellars
Sutter Home Winery
V. Sattui Winery

AUTUMN
Beaulieu Vineyard
Cakebread Cellars
Clos du Val
Robert Mondavi Winery
Mumm Napa Estates
St. Clement Vineyards
St. Supéry Vineyards and Winery
Trefethen Vineyards

WINERIES RECOMMENDED FOR YOUR SPECIAL INTERESTS

ATTENTION TO WINE WITH FOOD
Beringer Vineyards
Cakebread Cellars
Domaine Carneros
Domaine Chandon
Grgich Hills Cellar

Robert Mondavi Winery
Mumm Napa Estates
Niebaum-Coppola Estate Winery
Rutherford Hill Winery
St. Supéry Vineyards and Winery
Stag's Leap Wine Cellars
Sterling Vineyards
V. Sattui Winery

CAVES
Beringer Vineyards
Clos Pegase
Pride Mountain Vineyards
Rutherford Hill Winery
St. Clement Vineyards
Schramsberg Vineyards

CHAMPAGNE/ SPARKLING WINE
Artesa Winery
Beaulieu Vineyard
Domaine Carneros
Domaine Chandon
Robert Mondavi Winery
Mumm Napa Estates
Schramsberg Vineyards

CONTEMPORARY ART COLLECTIONS
Artesa Winery
Clos Pegase
The Hess Collection Winery
Robert Mondavi Winery
St. Supéry Vineyards and Winery
Silverado Vineyards

CONTEMPORARY OR SPECIAL ARCHITECTURE
Artesa Winery
Cakebread Cellars
Chimney Rock Winery
Clos Pegase
Frog's Leap Winery
The Hess Collection Winery
Robert Mondavi Winery
Joseph Phelps Vineyards
Rutherford Hill Winery
Sterling Vineyards

FRENCH CHATEAU– STYLE ARCHITECTURE
Chateau Montelena
Domaine Carneros
Niebaum-Coppola Estate Winery

GARDENS
Beringer Vineyards
Cakebread Cellars
Chateau Montelena
Chimney Rock Winery
Domaine Chandon
Frog's Leap Winery
Robert Mondavi Winery
Niebaum-Coppola Estate Winery
Joseph Phelps Vineyards
St. Clement Vineyards
Schramsberg Vineyards
Stag's Leap Wine Cellars
Sutter Home Winery
Trefethen Vineyards
V. Sattui Winery

OUTSTANDING PANORAMAS
Artesa Winery
Chateau Montelena
Chimney Rock Winery
Domaine Carneros
Niebaum-Coppola Estate Winery
Joseph Phelps Vineyards
Pride Mountain Vineyards
Rutherford Hill Winery
Silverado Vineyards
Sterling Vineyards

OUTSTANDING TOURS
Domaine Chandon
Frog's Leap Winery
Robert Mondavi Winery
Mumm Napa Estates
Pride Mountain Vineyards
St. Supéry Vineyards and Winery

PICNIC SETTINGS
Clos du Val
Clos Pegase
Pride Mountain Vineyards
V. Sattui Winery

SELF-TOURS
The Hess Collection Winery
St. Supéry Vineyards and Winery
Sterling Vineyards
Sutter Home Winery
V. Sattui Winery

STAINED GLASS WINDOWS
Beringer Vineyards
St. Clement Vineyards
Silverado Vineyards
Sterling Vineyards

VICTORIAN HOMES, INTERIORS
Beringer Vineyards
St. Clement Vineyards
St. Supéry Vineyards and Winery
Sutter Home Winery

VINEYARD TOURS
Cakebread Cellars
Chimney Rock Winery
Clos du Val
Frog's Leap Winery
Grgich Hills Cellar
Robert Mondavi Winery
Pride Mountain Vineyards
St. Supéry Vineyards and Winery
Trefethen Vineyards

WINE-MAKING EMPHASIS
Cakebread Cellars
Clos du Val
Domaine Carneros
Domaine Chandon
Grgich Hills Cellar
Robert Mondavi Winery
Mumm Napa Estates
St. Supéry Vineyards and Winery
Schramsberg Vineyards
Silverado Vineyards
Stag's Leap Wine Cellars
Trefethen Vineyards

TRIANGLE TOURS

Three winery tours per day—or fewer—is an ideal scheduling goal for an enjoyable stay in the Napa Valley. This takes into consideration a first tour starting around 10 A.M. and time for lunch at one of the many fine restaurants here or out of your own picnic hamper. Plan time to visit the towns as well, which offer museums, shopping, and historical attractions that should not be overlooked. Wineries close by 5:30 P.M. at the latest, allowing time to rest before the evening meal.

To the left, you'll find examples of day-trip winery destinations in geographically balanced "triangles." They're starting points for your imagination. These triangle tours do not take into account specific interests, such as a fascination with Victorian architecture or a passion for contemporary art or a yearning to visit gardens. (See recommendations according to these and other interests on pages 24–25.) Nor do they list specific restaurants in the various regions. For restaurant listings, check with the various magazines, newspapers, or chambers of commerce or turn to locals for friendly suggestions. I've suggested picnicking when one or more wineries in the optional triangle offers a comfortable picnic setting.

Remember that the valley's thirty-mile length means at least one hour of driving for a round-trip from either end, from Napa or Calistoga. This shortens the time for touring. You might consider mid-valley accommodations at one end of the valley one night and the opposite the next. Or zigzag through the valley, cutting through the vineyards on one of the lateral roads off Highway 29 or the Silverado Trail. Bear in mind that, even at its broadest point, the valley is only five miles wide.

Whatever your plans, relax and enjoy every minute of your stay.

THE
WINERIES

ARTESA WINERY

Artesa Winery
1345 Henry Road
Napa, CA 94559
(707) 224-1668
fax (707) 224-1672
Website: www.artesawinery.com
Email: info@artesawinery.com

Winemaker: Don Van Staaveren
Winery owner: Codorniu, S.A.

Access
Location: From Highway 29, turn west onto Highway 121 toward Sonoma. After 4 miles, turn right on Old Sonoma Road. After 1 block, turn left on Dealy Lane. Proceed northwest on Dealy Lane, which becomes Henry Road, where the road curves beyond Carneros Creek Winery. Turn left into the driveway.

Hours open for visits and tastings: 10 A.M.–5 P.M. daily.

Appointment necessary for tour? No, but groups of eight or more require a reservation. Complimentary tours at 11 A.M. and 2 P.M.

Wheelchairs accommodated? Yes.

Tastings
Charge for tasting with tour? Yes. Six 1-ounce tastes, $6; five reserve tastes (1 ounce), $10; Brut, $5 each glass; by the glass, ranges from $5–$12. Complimentary tours.
Charge for tasting without tour? As above.

Typical wines offered: Sparkling: Brut; still: Sauvignon Blanc, Chardonnay, Pinot Noir, Merlot, Cabernet Sauvignon, and Gewürztraminer.

Sales of wine-related items? Yes.

Picnics and Programs
Picnic area open to the public? No.

Special events or wine-related programs? Wine club.

The sleek, modern elements of Artesa Winery are hidden in the heart of a grassy Carneros hill, much like a James Bond hideout. This is one of Napa Valley's most architecturally contemporary wineries, designed to reproduce the form of a previously existing knoll in the Carneros vineyard region. Besides inflicting minimal impact on the countryside, the winery's design harmonizes—in fact meshes—with the surrounding landscape.

The Codorniu family of Barcelona owns this renamed winery, formerly known as Codorniu Napa. The family has produced wine since 1551 and was the first family in Spain to create *méthode champenoise* sparkling wine, in 1872. At this winery, still wines are now the predominant vintages, although some sparkling wines are made here as well. With such an ancient history, some might expect Moorish arches and Old World architecture for this, the first sparkling and still wine wine-making venture outside Spain for the Codorniu descendants. But, after an original five-year scouting of the grape-growing regions of the world, the decision was to buy land in Carneros and to build a sweepingly modern winery. The enterprise has drawn acclaim since its opening in 1991.

To reach the imposing property, you turn off Old Sonoma Road, very near Domaine Carneros. In fact, one suggestion is to visit both wineries back to back so that you can experience the variations in style—architectural as well as enological—between the French and Spanish companies.

On approaching the site, you may have difficulty identifying the estate until you reach the winery signs at the gates. Then comes the great "Aha!"

Yes, the winery is in view all along, but it blends so well with the surroundings that it appears to be one of the many other craggy hills in the area. Due as well to the native California matte fescue grasses planted on the earthen berm covering the facility, the winery hides its face. Once you are on the curving drive to the parking area at the base of the winery, the minimalist architecture by Spaniard Domingo Triay and Napa Valley architect E. R. Bouligny becomes a dominant force, which is sure to hold your attention throughout your stay.

A cascading waterfall cuts the center of the forty-five broad steps you will climb to reach Artesa's entry. The view seems to offer a new and better panorama at each landing during the ascent, culminating in the breathtaking vista from the top of the knoll. There you can see San Francisco Bay in the distance. Nearer is San Pablo Bay, which hugs the edges of Carneros, bringing with it the famous fog of the

region. The same view encompasses Millikin Peak and rolling hills and vineyards, including Artesa's 50 acres of vines (150 more acres lie on northern Alexander Valley property).

From the fountains playing at the winery's promontory, you will walk into the sophisticated silence of the winery. A rotating display of resident artist Gordon Huether's striking work decorates walls and corridors, and there is a "Carneros Concierge" center on the side of the tasting room. The concierge service will create a printout of other Carneros-region wineries, based on a questionnaire offered to visitors. Since Carneros is such a rapidly growing region, this is a useful service. There, surrounded by elegant wood

and metal interiors also designed by Triay, a tour guide will greet you warmly and lead you on a comprehensive tour. The guide will cover wine making and history, including a discussion of an ancient barrel and other wine-making artifacts brought from Barcelona. You will walk outside to the two tank presses, and then, inside, you will view several thousand French oak barrels as well as the still and sparkling wines bottling line where seventy-five thousand cases are bottled annually. Tours tend to be small in size; between six and ten visitors stroll with the guide. If you have entered via the handicapped access, expect some stairs on the tour. You will not actually descend four stories into the ground, but from an upper walkway you will see the aging sparkling wine on pallets.

There is something for everyone at this winery. You can choose to learn about the technical side of the winery or you may sit on the veranda, sip sparkling brut or a variety of still wines including Sauvignon Blanc, Chardonnay, Pinot Noir, Merlot, and Cabernet Sauvignon, and bask in the view.

The Spanish have a saying for it: *"¡Qué vida tan allegre!"*—What a happy life!

BEAULIEU VINEYARD

Beaulieu Vineyard
1960 St. Helena Highway
Rutherford, CA 94573
(707) 967-5200
fax (707) 963-5920
Website: www.bvwines.com
Email: bvinfo@bvwines.com

Winemaker: Joel Aiken
Winery owner: United Distillers &
Vintners (UDV)

Access
Location: On the corner of Rutherford
Road (Highway 128) and Highway 29.

Hours open for visits and tastings:
10 A.M.–5 P.M. daily, except major
holidays.

Appointment necessary for tour? No.

Wheelchairs accommodated? Yes.

Tastings
Charge for tasting with tour? Yes.
Complimentary wine on arrival; $5 for
five wines; Private Reserve Room $25
for five reserve wines, $10 for one.
Charge for tasting without tour?
As above.

Typical wines offered: Sauvignon Blanc,
Chardonnay, Cabernet Sauvignon,
Pinot Noir, and Merlot. Also wine
tasting at the Reserve Room.

Sales of wine-related items? Yes,
including logo glasses ($3 and $4.95).

Picnics and Programs
Picnic area open to the public? No.

Special events or wine-related
programs? Beaulieu Wine Society—
members' discounts on wine at winery
and by mail, as well as VIP tour and
tasting at winery, with advance reser-
vation, and various special events.

You can learn a tremendous amount about wine making at Beaulieu Vineyard even before the tour begins. On entering the barrel-shaped upper level of the visitors' center of this venerable winery, you'll be handed a glass of wine as welcome. Take your time to walk around the space, then join a tour. The tour guide leads you across the shaded parking area to the crush pad behind the winery, which was greatly enlarged in 1969 when members of the original Georges de Latour family sold Beaulieu to Heublein, Inc. During crush, you're at winemaker level watching grapes rain into the steel crush pads, which resemble huge metal V-shaped troughs. Perhaps because of the friendliness between the guides and the winery workers, there is very little sense of a huge corporation here. Although there are relatively few cellar workers year-round, 400 to 450 pickers are needed at harvest time and production yields nearly a million cases per year.

Next on the tour agenda, the group, which can vary in size from five to about twenty-five, is led to the "Valley of the Redwoods"—the area of the winery where traditional eighty-five-year-old redwood tanks create an aromatic wooden alley. Be sure to note the glass tubing running along the cement walls. With this system, fermented grape juice is pumped in a visible manner from one part of the winery to another, banding the cement stone walls with deep red or pale green, depending on the juices. You'll hear the bottling line activity in the background.

André Tchelistcheff, the revered active winemaker for the winery from 1938 until 1973, stamped his legendary mark on Beaulieu wines. It was he who created the distinguishing hallmark of BV wines by putting the juice of the vineyard into American, rather than French, oak barrels.

The actual winery faces Highway 29, with a wall of ivy and Virginia creeper covering the original brick and concrete building. It dates from 1885 and was owned by Seneca Ewer, one of the prominent landowners who joined the first circle of Napa Valley winemakers. Ewer's sale of the winery to Frenchman Georges de Latour was a fortuitous move for the history of wine making in the Napa Valley, as Latour was an extremely zealous entrepreneur who extended word of his winery (named *beau lieu*, French for "beautiful place") through San Francisco social circles, making the wine a turn-of-the-century favorite.

The tour ends back at the visitors' center with a generous tasting of Beaulieu wines and the option of tasting older wines in the Private Reserve Room. There, 1-ounce pours of such vintages as Reserve Chardonnay, Reserve Pinot Noir, 1990 or 1991 Georges de Latour, Tapestry and a more current Georges de Latour are sold at twenty-five dollars for all wines or ten dollars for one—a bargain, considering that these wines would normally sell for up to one hundred dollars per bottle.

Beringer Vineyards
2000 Main Street
St. Helena, CA 94574
(707) 963-7115
fax (707) 963-1735
Website: www.beringer.com
Email: See website

Winemaker: Ed Sbragia
Winery owner: Beringer Blass Wine
Estates

Access
Location: At the north end of St. Helena
on the left-hand side of Highway 29
(Main Street).

Hours open for visits and tastings:
10 A.M.–5 P.M. June 1–October 31;
10 A.M.–4 P.M. November 1–May 31,
except New Year's Day, Easter,
Thanksgiving, and Christmas.

Appointment necessary for tour? Yes,
for some; call first.

Wheelchairs accommodated? Yes.

Tastings
Charge for tasting with tour? $5 per
person (gratis for those under 21,
when accompanied by an adult).
Charge for tasting without tour?
$3–$10. Reserve tasting fee is
deductible from price of purchased
wine.

Typical wines offered: Complimentary
tasting of Napa Valley Chardonnay,
White Zinfandel, and Cabernet
Sauvignon. Private Reserve Room
tastings may include Private Reserve
and Sbragia Limited Release
Chardonnays, Private Release Cabernet
Sauvignon, Knight's Valley Cabernets,
Alluvium, and Howell Mountain Merlot.

Sales of wine-related items? Yes.

Picnics and Programs
Picnic area open to the public? No.

Special events or wine-related
programs? Special seasonal tours and
release events; wine club.

BERINGER VINEYARDS

At Beringer, you can visit an elegant Victorian home, photograph seasonal flower beds, or explore century-old tunnels for wine aging. This winery has generated vintages since 1876, earning it the title of Napa Valley's oldest winery with continuous production. Even during Prohibition, the Beringer family was granted approval to produce sacramental and medicinal wines and brandies when other companies closed their doors. Because of its lengthy history and recognition, hundreds of thousands of tourists have journeyed to the valley with Beringer as their specific goal.

On turning onto the estate grounds, you will first see the impressive seventeen-room Rhine House, built in the 1880s. The Beringer brothers—businessman Frederick and winemaker Jacob—built the home to resemble their birthplace in Mainz, Germany. The slate roof, European stained glass windows, and intricately inlaid wooden floors are all original, as is most of the home, which was restored after 1971 when the winery was purchased by Nestlé, Inc. Then, under ownership of the Texas Pacific Group, the winery became a publicly traded company in 1997; it is now owned by Beringer Blass Wine Estates, with Australian interests behind it.

The walk south from the parking lot will lead you past the Hudson House, Jacob's home, where he, his wife, and their six children lived. It now houses Beringer's private dining room for special winery and culinary events. Visitors usually find the spring-flowering wisteria, azaleas, oleanders, and roses on the Beringer grounds unforgettable. If photography is your hobby, be sure to have film for this visit. Visitors who don't choose to follow the tour may enjoy a tasting in either the Old Bottling Room or the Private Reserve Room.

Due to the popularity of this winery tour, delays may be frequent. However, tours begin every half-hour from the promenade in front of the restored Old Winery. Tickets can be purchased in the Carriage House visitors' center below the Old Winery, adjacent to the parking lot.

Outside the Old Winery, the tour guide reviews the history of the Beringer family and the winery. The tour continues into the Old Winery with a brief discussion of basic wine production methods as well as ideal storage and cellaring conditions. You'll learn of the Chinese laborers who were hired to chisel a thousand feet of tunnels from the Spring Mountain foothills just west of the Hudson House. On that site,

Jacob oversaw the construction of a gravity-flow winery, 104 feet long by 40 feet wide (now the Old Winery). It was completed in 1876. Although Beringer now makes wine in a more modern facility directly across Highway 29, some of the renowned Cabernet Sauvignons are aged in French oak barrels within Jacob's original tunnels. Don't miss the hand-carved German barrels dating back 150 years.

The tour meanders through the tunnels, which have been restructured for seismic purposes but still impart a sense of the original cellars. There is even a wine library, which houses vintages as old as 1937, dusty with time.

Want to get close to the grapevines? There are special tours of the home vineyard, including a barrel tasting.

Down in the main gardens, the "Leaning Oak" holds forth in a prominent corner. Branches of the massive deciduous oak tree curl back on each other like a corkscrew. Some tour guides say that the roots of the two-hundred-plus-year-old tree stretched under the caves and up into barrels of wine to cause the tree's contorted form.

The last stop on the Beringer tour is in the Old Winery and its gift shop that stands on the hill behind the Rhine House and the Hudson House. There you will taste three wines.

Following the tour and tasting, you might choose to stroll through the Rhine House, which is open for casual viewing. There you can taste reserve wines in the Private Reserve Room on the main level of Frederick Beringer's home and view the stunning stained glass windows there. Beringer holds the finest stained glass collection in the Napa Valley. Insurance coverage on the Rhine House alone is now more than six million dollars, a far cry from the original twenty-eight-thousand-dollar construction costs for the entire Germanic Victorian. The main rooms of the home are open for inspection, including an upper bedroom now dubbed the Founders' Room, where special reserve wines are poured.

Guides at Beringer are the only ones in the valley to toast visitors as they taste wine. "To your health!" or "Have a great time in the valley!" are frequent salutes, accompanied by clinking glasses. Guests are encouraged to drink wine at home, even with simple family fare. By the time you walk back to the parking area, you'll have a deeper understanding of Victorian times, a view to the future of wine making, and an understanding of how wine making related to life then as well as now.

Cakebread Cellars
8300 St. Helena Highway
Rutherford, CA 94573
(800) 588-0298
fax (707) 967-4012
Website: www.cakebread.com
Email: cellars@cakebread.com

Winemaker: Julianne Laks
Winery owners: Cakebread family

Access
Location: Take Highway 29 to about a quarter-mile north of Robert Mondavi Winery; look for stone walls and colorful flower beds.

Hours open for visits and tastings: 10 A.M.–4 P.M. daily, except New Year's Day, Easter, Thanksgiving, and Christmas.

Appointment necessary for tour? Yes; call 24 hours in advance or early the same morning. Tours at 10:30 A.M. and 2 P.M.

Wheelchairs accommodated? Yes.

Tastings
Charge for tasting with tour? No.
Charge for tasting without tour? $5 for three wines; $10 for five wines.

Typical wines offered: Current vintages of Sauvignon Blanc, Chardonnay, Merlot, Pinot Noir, Rubaiyat (proprietary blend), and Cabernet Sauvignon. Two reserve wines: Benchland Select and Three Sisters Cabernet Sauvignon.

Sales of wine-related items? Yes.

Picnics and Programs
Picnic area open to the public? No.

Special events or wine-related programs? Educational cooking classes with wine pairing.

CAKEBREAD CELLARS

Among the myriad wineries along the road between Napa and Calistoga, Cakebread Cellars stands out in a colorful way. In any season of the year, look for masses of flowers in bloom on the east side of the road in Rutherford, just about halfway along the thirty-mile stretch.

The exuberance of the flowers is mirrored in the strong family spirit that greets all visitors. A joyful work ethic has been passed from winery founders Jack and Dolores Cakebread to their children and on to the winery staff, and through them to winery visitors.

The winery tour starts in the vineyard. There the informative, low-key tour opens with talk of the importance of the right land to grow the best grapes. "At an average cost of two hundred thousand dollars an acre or more, Napa Valley floor land is the second most expensive farm soil in the United States," notes the tour guide, who is swift to mention that the most expensive farmland is in Riverside, California. He notes that grapes are second only to cotton in agricultural importance to the state of California, where 75 percent of the nation's wine grapes, 90 percent of its table grapes, and 100 percent of its raisin grapes are grown. "But all the vineyards combined in the Napa Valley grow only 4 percent of those wine grapes, and the first cash crop of grapes doesn't mature until four

to five years after the rootstock is planted," he says, putting a realistic note on the thousands of rows of vines stretching the width of the valley.

There are now about four hundred wineries in the Napa Valley, but when Jack Cakebread decided to plant grapes in 1973, his winery license was number thirty-eight. At the time, he and his wife bought land just north of Oakville from elderly friends named Sturdivant, with the understanding that the friends could live out their days on the property. Then, when the Cakebreads came on board, they created a true mom-and-pop operation, with mechanical know-how and a strong sense of design from Jack and culinary savvy with a nutritious slant from Dolores. They frequently travel to promote their Cabernet Sauvignon, Sauvignon Blanc, and Chardonnay.

Although the winery has grown from its early stages to a seventy-two-acre property with production of fifty thousand cases a year, it retains the hands-on feeling and remains a family project. Son Bruce is now the president of the winery; Dennis works as business manager for the company; and third son Steven, an executive for an electronics firm in Singapore, is a member of the board of directors for the winery. Dolores has developed a culinary program for visiting chefs and wine writers to encourage them to be aware

of local produce and other Napa Valley food resources and how to pair them with wine. Also, she oversees the floral welcome at the winery's entrance.

"This is a working winery. Please stay together as we tour the production area," admonishes the tour guide as you join a group of ten visitors in the air-conditioned building. The winery buildings, designed by William Turnbull, present a contemporary redwood barn architecture that blends easily into the landscape. Engineering buffs are intrigued with the ultramodern equipment, which offers such practical systems as a drainage process that allows a simultaneous hosing of machines, vats, walls, and floors, as well as an air-flow program that reduces electrical costs.

In the storage room, instructions for how to read notations, the brand marks and pencil jottings on a wine barrel, are clearly explained. "Here," says the tour guide, pointing to one end of a barrel, "is the barrel maker's name. This notes the source of the wood. Next, the year the barrel was bought, followed by the wine initials [C.S. for Cabernet Sauvignon, for example] and finally the vintage and any special comments, such as ML for malolactic fermentation."

The guide fields all questions, such as how the winemaker balances the oak influences in flavoring the fermented grape juice. "Believe me," he says, "the last thing we want is wine with the flavor of Chateau Two-by-Four! Too much wood can be a real negative for wines that are made to lay down a long while."

There is no pressure to return to the tasting room, though most do so readily. Most tourists have gone out of their way to visit Cakebread for specific reasons, such as to tour the source of a bottle of wine opened to celebrate their anniversary or at their favorite restaurant. One tourist said, "It's nice to find out that the Cakebreads are real people who like their wine and their work . . . and beautiful flowers."

CHATEAU MONTELENA

Chateau Montelena
1429 Tubbs Lane
Calistoga, CA 94515
(707) 942-5105
fax (707) 942-4221
Website: www.montelena.com
Email: reservations@montelena.com

Winemaker: James P. "Bo" Barrett
Winery owner: James L. Barrett,
managing general partner

Access
Location: Two miles north of the
intersection of Highway 29 and Lincoln
Avenue in Calistoga; turn east (right if
driving north) onto Tubbs Lane.
Chateau Montelena is past Old Faithful
Geyser, on the north. Look for large
gates.

Hours open for visits and tastings:
9:30 A.M.– 4 P.M. daily, except major
holidays and the third Saturday in May.

Appointment necessary for tour? Yes.
Tours at 9:30 A.M. and 1:30 P.M.

Wheelchairs accommodated? Yes,
except in unpaved parking lot.

Tastings
Charge for tasting with tour? $25,
including sit-down tasting of five
wines. The tour takes 1^1/$_2$–2 hours.
Charge for tasting without tour?
$10 for three wines.

Typical wines offered: Chardonnay,
Riesling, Cabernet Sauvignon, and
Zinfandel.

Sales of wine-related items? Yes.

Picnics and Programs
Picnic area open to the public? No.

Special events or wine-related
programs? No.

In the manner of the faithful geyser up the road from Chateau Montelena, a discrete, major spurt in the wine world brought this Napa Valley winery to prominence. That burst of energy came in June 1976, when for the first time, the wines of California overcame the grapes of Gaul. During a critical blind tasting judged in Paris by nine French oenophiles, California wines topped those of France, with Chateau Montelena '73 as the champion Chardonnay.

The judges could not have been more amazed. What might have surprised them as well is that this winery is housed in a building of truly Gallic origins. Designed after the great chateaux of Bordeaux and built by a French architect, this was one of the small, thriving wineries of the early 1900s. Winery walls are three to twelve feet thick, made of imported and native cut stone. Senator Alfred Tubbs, originally a Bostonian, was the owner who chose the French design of what was then the sixth-largest winery in the valley.

The rustic redwood tasting room that you'll see on arrival gives little hint of the splendid chateau beneath it. The visitors' room is located on an upper floor in the rear of the chateau, but appreciation of the tradition and architecture of this winery demands making the short walk downhill, to properly view the ivy-covered stone façade of this elegant estate. There is a splendid vista point from man-made Jade Lake, which fronts the chateau. From there, you'll view the chateau, the willow-framed lake, and the quaint red lacquered bridge that spans the lake from the shore to island pavilions.

Beyond the lake lie acres of Chateau Montelena vineyards, the home of Jim Barrett—who dubs himself a "caretaker of the land" instead of its owner—and Mount St. Helena, rising four thousand feet in the background. Some say this is the Napa Valley dream view; it is definitely a photo opportunity to consider seriously. Wildlife aficionados will find ducks, swans, turtles, catfish, and a number of wild birds using the lake and island as a sanctuary. Considering the heady floral perfume that laces summer's hot, dry air, thoughts of Monet's garden at Giverny may jump to mind. Cascading old-fashioned roses vie with flora and fauna in the full spectrum of colors and bouquets.

In fact, there is a similar idyllic quality to time spent chez Monet and at this winery.

Along one of the lakeside paths is a plaque proclaiming an ancient Chinese proverb: "Peace and tranquility to all who enter here." The aphorism was placed by former owners Yort and Jeanne Frank, who lived in the chateau after Prohibition forced closure of the business. Now the chateau is used for winery purposes only. Present owner Barrett, whose son Bo is winemaker, offers the same four varietals today as in 1972: Cabernet Sauvignon, Zinfandel, Chardonnay, and Riesling. Barrett says his background as an attorney gave him the proper perspective on a life in the wine industry: "I spent eighteen years giving pain to people," he explains. "Now I spend my life giving them pleasure."

Pleasure they do receive. During a post-tour tasting, a visitor from Miami explained that she particularly enjoys the winery's Riesling, which is sold only in-house, because "it's not high in tannin that would make me want a drink after I've had a drink."

And what of the famous Chateau Montelena Chardonnay, made with grapes grown in volcanic and sedimentary souls in the Oak Knoll district of Napa Valley? It is still one of the most popular wines tasted and purchased at the winery, years after the touted Paris tasting, and second only to the Montelena Estate Cabernet Sauvignon.

Wine is not all that visitors take with them on departing the chateau. One tour guide notes, "Most people come like pilgrims to taste the Chardonnay or Cabernet, and when they get here, the beauty of the place adds to the whole experience and they leave refreshed."

CHIMNEY ROCK WINERY

Chimney Rock Winery
5350 Silverado Trail
Napa, CA 94558
(800) 257-2641
fax (707) 257-2036
Website: www.chimneyrock.com
Email: club@chimneyrock.com

Winemaker: Douglas Fletcher
Winery owners: Terlato family of the
Terlato Wine Group (TWG)

Access
Location: Five miles north of Napa on
the Silverado Trail in the Stags Leap
District.

Hours open for visits and tastings:
10 A.M.–5 P.M. daily, except Easter,
Thanksgiving, and Christmas.

Appointment necessary for tour? Yes.

Wheelchairs accommodated? Yes.

Tastings
Charge for tasting with tour? $20.
Charge for tasting without tour? $7,
including a souvenir glass.

Typical wines offered: Fumé Blanc,
Rosé of Cabernet Franc, Chardonnay,
and current and older vintages of
Cabernet Sauvignon and Elevago.

Sales of wine-related items? Yes.

Picnics and Programs
Picnic area open to the public? No.

Special events or wine-related
programs? Wine club.

The iron gates that open onto Chimney Rock's driveway point the way to one of Napa Valley's more splendid views. Your eye moves from the valley floor up to the eastern hillside, where trellised vineyards stretch along the undulating earth. With or without leaves, the rows of vines follow the various curves and openings in the land. The property seems to stretch forever.

To the right of the entry road, the winery and hospitality center welcome guests for tours. Even though reservations are required, visitors are welcome to join weekday tours of the seventeenth-century-style Cape Dutch buildings. An interesting twist on wine tasting is that you'll be offered a glass of the winery's Chardonnay and Fumé Blanc before tour departure, with the suggestion to "bring along your glass as we walk." This touch enhances the feeling that visitors are sauntering about a gracious home, the goal of original owners Hack and Stella Wilson and a tradition now continued by the Tony Terlato family.

The South African Huguenot style of the Cape Dutch property is unique in the Napa Valley. The graceful roofline curves are particularly visible from the road before early summer, when the poplars that line the estate act as leafless sentinels, giving a full view of the various buildings on the estate.

The tour starts at the hearth in the well-lit entry room. Antique fireplace tools decorate the white walls. Occasionally the tour will include a visit to the private tasting room, where an imposing seventeenth-century highboy from South Africa dominates one white wall. That and the other blanched walls of the hospitality center contrast with the rich tones of antique wooden tables, light fixtures, and accent pieces adorning the space. The chalky walls are a refreshing change from the more typical use of unadorned wood in wineries built in the Napa Valley over the last thirty years.

The tour moves outside to a shaded area where sunken waterfalls divide part of the generous patio. From there you'll have a full view of the frieze mounted atop the winery's back wall. The subject of this nine-by-thirty-eight-foot work of art is Ganymede, cup bearer to the gods. The eighteenth-century German sculptor Anton Anreith created the original for the Groot Constantia winery at the Cape Colony of Africa, where Anreith was employed by the Dutch East India Company. To duplicate the masterpiece for Chimney Rock, the Wilsons commissioned California sculptor Michael Casey, resident restoration artist for the state capitol in Sacramento. Imagine mounting the fiberglass-reinforced concrete duplication, which weighs five tons!

Moving to the vineyards and then to the winery, you'll soon realize that this is one of the valley's small wineries. With few full-time employees, chances are strong that you'll meet Doug Fletcher, the winemaker, and that you'll be able to speak with him about his wines, which are made strictly in the French manner. Cabernet Sauvignon, Merlot, Cabernet Franc, and

Petit Verdot grapes are all used to create Bordeaux-style wines.

If you feel misty while tasting the wine, the cause might be the winery's *faux cave* system, which creates constant humidity by spraying a fine fog over the thousand aging barrels, which will yield fifteen thousand cases of wine.

As Cabernet Sauvignon and other vintages are served at the wine-tasting bar, the story is recounted of how friendship with wine expert Alexis Lichine led the late Hack Wilson—a former hotelier and soft drink and beer marketer—to his 1980 purchase of 185 acres in the Stags Leap District, including the Chimney Rock Golf Course. Until 2001, nine holes of the golf course remained on the property, but the Terlatos, Wilsons, and Fletcher transformed that ideal wine-growing fifty-acre plot to Cabernet Sauvignon vineyards and constructed a second onsite winery facility. They planted vineyards based on Lichine's dictate to "look at all of the regions, but when you buy, buy in Napa Valley, for Napa is to California what Bordeaux is to France."

Some would say they scored a hole-in-one by doing so.

43

Clos du Val
5330 Silverado Trail
Napa, CA 94558
(707) 259-2225
fax (707) 252-6125
Website: www.closduval.com
Email: cdv@closduval.com

Winemakers: Bernard Portet,
John Clews, and Kian Tavakoli
Winery owners: John Goelet and family

Access
Location: Five miles north of city of
Napa on the east side of the Silverado
Trail.

Hours open for visits and tastings:
10 A.M.–5 P.M. daily, except New Year's
Day, Easter, Thanksgiving, and
Christmas.

Appointment necessary for tour? Yes;
call one to two days in advance.

Wheelchairs accommodated? Yes.

Tastings
Charge for tasting with tour?
Complimentary with tour for individu-
als. For groups, $10 per person.
Charge for tasting without tour? $5 for
four to five wines or complimentary
with wine purchase.

Typical wines offered: Chardonnay,
Cabernet Sauvignon, Pinot Noir,
Zinfandel, and Merlot.

Sales of wine-related items? Yes.

Picnics and Programs
Picnic area open to the public? Yes,
with appointment.

Special events or wine-related
programs? Yes. The Cellar Club and
special wine-related parties through-
out the year open to all, including
Cellar Club members.

CLOS DU VAL

The massive doors to the Clos du Val tasting room open to a cool visitors' room, a wel- come contrast to the hundred-degree heat of a Napa Valley summer day. This room touts a twenty-eight-foot ceiling and a feeling of space to match the size of the front doors. Here you'll find a collection of vintages since 1972 and friendly people proud of their work.

It is from the cavernous tasting room that tours depart, directly to the vineyards. This is a winery seri- ously involved with the land and in explaining the annual struggle with the soil to produce top-quality grapes. Tours are usually small—two to eight people— and they cover all stages of viticulture and enology.

The view from the vineyards, the tourists' first stop, is exceptional: you are surrounded by acres of vineyards, many edged with roses.

"See those roses?" asked one Clos du Val tour guide, pointing to rosebushes laden with red and yel- low blossoms. "There is a Bordeaux tradition that says if the roses bear many blossoms, there will be a strong harvest." This is one explanation for the roses seen frequently bordering vineyards. An alternate explanation is that the buds act like canaries in a coal mine; if the birds weaken, miners take heed and head

for a safer area. In this case, if the roses droop or show signs of disease, the grower inspects the soil or rootstock for disease. Both rose stories have their roots in France, as does Bernard Portet, the winery's first winemaker. Portet is the son of the former *régisseur* of Chateau Lafite, and he instills his love of French oak by insisting on French Nevers and Allier oak barrels for aging wine. The Cabernets are kept in oak for about two years.

The vineyard tour takes you right to the soil that was once a lava bed. If you want to walk between the vines, you will. This is not a dainty sandal tour, unless you don't mind shaking out a few pebbles. If the grapes are at an edible stage, be assured you'll taste some.

Moving from the vineyards, you'll learn of the Clos du Val lands dotting various regions of the Napa Valley: Stags Leap District (where the winery is situated); State Lane, in Yountville; and the Carneros region. Cabernet Sauvignon, Merlot, Zinfandel, Semillon, Cabernet Franc, Pinot Noir, and Chardonnay grapes are bases for the Clos du Val wines, as well as Sangiovese under the Tre Grazie label.

If you happen to visit in the early summer, you may be able to view ice on the outside of the stainless-

residue at the bottom of wine bottles—those "flakes" are often tartrates. They're not harmful, but they are not attractive, and this is why many wineries follow the practice of freezing, followed by light filtration.

For an unusual diversion, watch the barrel cleaner in action. When needed, it is fixed on the floor in an alley between layers of barrels. When a high-pressure sprinkler is turned on inside the barrel, the barrel spins as if by magic. This is a reminder of the frivolously entertaining mechanical water gardens outside of Salzburg, but on a practical level.

The tour guide offers an excellent explanation of how to "read" a barrel and, more importantly for the home consumer, how to read a wine label. The latter instruction takes place back at the wine tasting bar in the visitors' center. While there, you may also hear about Taltarni Vineyards in Australia. That is due to the fact that the same owner, John Goelet, owns both properties. Dominique Portet, the brother of Clos du Val's winemaker Bernard, was the former winemaker in Australia.

While enjoying the various wines, don't miss the collection of droll cartoons lightening the subject of wine. These full-color, framed originals by Ronald Searle hang on a wall near the huge entry doors. They were commissioned by John Goelet. I have observed tourists, glass of wine in hand, reading the cartoon wall and laughing out loud, thus enjoying two of life's finest pleasures at once. Three, if you count visiting the Napa Valley.

steel fermenters, indicating Ariadne, Clos du Val's Chardonnay, is being cold-stabilized, a process pioneered at Clos du Val.

Just in case all this discussion leaves you out in the cold, a few words from winemaker Portet about how cold stabilization works: "We drop the wine temperature to twenty-eight degrees and leave it there so tartrate crystals will precipitate out here in the winery and not in the bottle at home." You may have seen

CLOS PEGASE

Clos Pegase
1060 Dunaweal Lane
Calistoga, CA 94515
(707) 942-4981
fax (707) 942-4993
Website: www.clospegase.com
Email: info@clospegase.com

Winemaker: Shaun Richardson
Winery owners: Jan and Mitsuko Shrem

Access

Location: On Highway 29, 7 miles north of St. Helena, turn northeast (right, if driving north from St. Helena) at Dunaweal Lane. The winery is on the left after 0.7 miles, across from the entrance to Sterling Vineyards.

Hours open for visits and tastings: 10:30 A.M.–5 P.M. daily, except New Year's Day, Thanksgiving, Christmas Eve, and Christmas.

Appointment necessary for tour? No. Tours at 11 A.M. and 2 P.M.

Wheelchairs accommodated? Yes.

Tastings

Charge for tasting with tour? No fee for tour. $5 for white wines; $7.50 for reds; $20 for Hommage (a meritage wine) tasting.
Charge for tasting without tour? As above.

Typical wines offered: Chardonnay, Sauvignon Blanc, Cabernet Sauvignon, Merlot, Pinot Blanc, Cabernet Franc, Hommage, and Port.

Sales of wine-related items? Yes.

Picnics and Programs

Picnic area open to the public? Yes, picnic tables available—first come, first serve.

Special events or wine-related programs? Contact the Events Department, (707) 942-4981, ext. 281. Jan Shrem's Wine & Art presentation is on the third Saturday of every month at 2:00 P.M., except in December and January–gratis, no reservation needed.

Clos Pegase is a haven for lovers of art and antiquities. A visit to the winery demonstrates the lengths to which owners Jan and Mitsuko Shrem have gone to create a showplace for their Cabernets, Chardonnays, and other wines.

Before zeroing in on the final design of their winery, the owners initiated a national architectural design competition sponsored by the San Francisco Museum of Modern Art. The winery opened in 1987. Since then, Clos Pegase has garnered numerous international awards for its architect, Princeton University professor Michael Graves. His winning design, a Greco-Roman temple to wine and the arts, makes an impressive statement from the moment you drive onto the estate. Contemporary sculpture in the parking lot says it all: art reigns here. In fact, for frequent Clos Pegase visitors the tour guide will point out the latest additions to the collection, such as Jacques Lipschitz's *Bellerophon Taming Pegasus,* Henry Moore's *Mother Earth,* Cesare Peverelli's *The Urban Gent,* or the giant bronze thumb by Cesar that rises out of the vineyards abutting the winery property.

Guests are welcome to sit on the grounds to picnic, according to Jan Shrem. "I want people to feel the connection between wine, food, and the arts," he says with a sweeping gesture of his hand.

Various public rooms at the winery run the gamut from the Harvest Room, thus named due to giant enlargements of vineyard scenes from the medieval *Book of Hours* that adorn the walls, to well-lit caves lined with ancient Bacchanalian statuary. It is in one of the caves that Shrem offers the public a monthly slide show of wine as it has been depicted in art over four thousand years.

While strolling from the tasting room through the winery caves and back again, tourists can't miss informative boards with key wine-in-art works related to wine in portraiture; wine in mythology; wine and religion; wine as a love potion; wine and the still life; and wine vessels, from the ancient to the contemporary.

Watch for these other outstanding features while on tour:

- The winemaker's laboratory, a little masterpiece of practical contemporary architecture and built-in cabinetry bathed in northeastern light.
- The three-hundred-year-old oak tree framed by the two axes of the winery.
- Terra-cotta tiles covering the winery's floor, lending unity with the Greco-Roman building style; there's even a wine gutter cut into the tiles along the tasting room floor.

- The tall barrels beyond the tasting room window wall, reproductions of wine-aging vats found in ancient Roman drawings; they were constructed of French oak in the United States.
- The massive single column that dominates the entrance to the winery. Is it supportive or purely an artistic statement?

A number of visitors are curious about the winery's name. Why Pegasus as a "mascot"? Shrem's response is that he and his wife wished to reflect the mythological beginnings of wine. According to the legends, Pegasus, the winged horse of Greek mythology, gave birth to wine and the arts when his hooves brushed the earth, unleashing the sacred spring of the Muses. The springwaters tapped roots of the vines and thus inspired the artists and poets who drank the fruit of the vine.

Clos in French, connotes any enclosed space. As a Napa Valley winery, Clos Pegase is not just any enclosed space—it is unique.

DOMAINE CARNEROS

Domaine Carneros
1240 Duhig Road
Napa, CA 94559
(707) 257-0101
fax (707) 257-3020
Website: www.domainecarneros.com
Email: See website

Winemaker: Eileen Crane
Winery owners: Champagne Taittinger,
Kobrand, and other American partners

Access
Location: At the point of Highway
121/12 at Duhig Road, 4 miles south-
west of the city of Napa.

Hours open for visits and tastings:
10 A.M.–6 P.M. daily, except New Year's
Day, Thanksgiving, and Christmas.

Appointment necessary for tour? No,
except for groups of ten or more. For
large groups, contact (707) 257-0101,
ext. 122. Tours begin at 10:15 A.M.
and are on the hour 11 A.M.–4 P.M.

Wheelchairs accommodated? Yes.

Tastings
Charge for tasting with tour? $4.25
to $10 per 4-ounce glass.
Charge for tasting without tour?
As above.

Typical wines offered: Sparkling: Le
Rêve Blanc de Blancs, Brut, and Rosé;
still: Famous Gate Pinot Noir, DC Pinot
Noir, and Avant Garde Pinot Noir.

Sales of wine-related items? Yes.

Picnics and Programs
Picnic area open to the public? No.

Special events or wine-related
programs? By appointment (ext. 122).

The classic elegance of the eighteenth-century chateau that houses Domaine Carneros's sparkling-wine-making facility draws instant attention from travelers in the southwestern tip of the Carneros District of the Napa Valley. Here, in an area frequently blanketed by fog from nearby San Pablo Bay, the modern castle presides on a hill at the vineyard edge. Among American vineyards, it is an international nexus.

Domaine Carneros itself is a partnership of the Champagne Taittinger house of Reims, France, as well as Kobrand Corporation and other partners. The grapes, grown immediately to the north, are used in making Winery Lake and Sterling vintages for Seagram's, the Canadian spirits company. Spain holds forth behind the di Rosa property: almost out of view due to its minimalist architecture, Artesa's profile hints to those who search the hills. Finally, south of Domaine Carneros lie the Swiss vineyards of Cuvaison.

Since the first infusion of French funds into the area, with the purchase of Domaine Chandon in 1973, the Napa Valley has seen more construction and growth owing to its international support. In most cases, the recently built wineries have demonstrated modern architectural styling. But in the case of Domaine Carneros this is not so.

The winery is patterned after the Taittinger-owned Chateau de la Marquetterie in Champagne. Seventy-two steps, broken by occasional landings, lead to the broad stone terrace and entry of the winery. (There is a clearly designated secondary entrance for those intimidated by the stairway.) Once inside, the first impression is of the grandeur of the place: high ceilings, a graceful staircase, and well-appointed furnishings balance with local limestone and French marble floors.

Follow your eyes into the tasting room at the north wing of the "chateau." It is there that you will join a tour group to see the inner workings of the winery, as well as to learn the background on the French link with Domaine Carneros.

"The fireplace mantel is a Louis XVI piece brought from France, as is this painting of Madame de Pompadour, mistress of Louis XV," says the tour guide. The story goes that a fortune-teller alerted Madame de Pompadour's father that his daughter was to be the mistress of the king. As a result, the gentleman trained his daughter for life in court. That meant he made certain she knew how to read and write in order to mesh easily with the literate lords and ladies of Louis XV's inner circle. This painting, which commands the foyer and which formerly hung at the Hotel Crillon in Paris, depicts Madame de Pompadour with books and sheet music.

From that historical discussion, you will move into a video presentation about the vineyard year for Pinot Noir and Chardonnay, the two grapes ideal for sparkling wine. An excellent segment explains the budding process used on the rootstock. At the video's

conclusion, the wide screen is raised, and behind a large window you will see a "forest" of stainless-steel fermentation tanks, a practical extension of the wine-making procedures covered on film.

From there, a short staircase leads down to a viewing platform from which the guide will point out the continuing stages of *méthode champenoise*, the double-fermentation sparkling-wine process that creates effervescence in the wine. This includes riddling, which is done primarily by mechanical methods despite winemaker Eileen Crane's inclusion of hand-riddling at the winery. You'll also see the disgorging-dosage-corking-cleaning-neck-foiling-labeling-bottling line, which is extremely modern equipment in comparison with the antique bottlers on display on the platform.

"Remember," laughs the guide, "the lower the alcohol content, the lower the calories—and sparkling wine has a total of only 12 percent alcohol. I call it a sumptuous diet drink!"

As the group follows along, they learn that ultraviolet light prematurely ages sparkling wine,

which is why the aging area—where the wine is aged twenty months—is rather dimly lit. Because the winery was built on top of a knoll, the temperature in the underground aging area simulates cave temperature. This architectural technique frequently is employed to reduce air-conditioning costs as much as to effect cavelike conditions.

In the design of this opulent setting, even the rest rooms received detailed attention. These are the best-appointed rest rooms in the valley.

Back upstairs, Domaine Carneros wine is sold by the glass or by the bottle, accompanied by tasty appetizers. Despite formal surroundings, the tasting-room staff is warm and genial.

There is a sense of the civilized life that arises from sitting on French-style chairs, listening to classical music, and sipping Napa Valley sparkling wine, overlooking the hills of Carneros. Whether you visit wearing jeans or summer finery, be prepared to feel like royalty.

DOMAINE CHANDON

Domaine Chandon
1 California Drive
Yountville, CA 94599
(707) 944-2280
fax (707) 944-1123
Website: www.chandon.com
Email: info@chandon.com

Winemaker: Wayne Donaldson
Winery owner: Moët-Hennessey–Louis
Vuitton

Access

Location: Off Highway 29 at Yountville.
From the Veterans Home exit, go west
on California Drive; turn right into
entrance drive.

Hours open for visits and tastings:
Visitors' center is open 10 A.M.–6 P.M.
daily. The restaurant is open
Thursday–Monday. Lunch is served
11:30 A.M.–2 P.M.; dinner is served
6–9 P.M.

Appointment necessary for tour? No,
except for groups of fifteen or more.
During harvest, tours are offered on the
hour, 11 A.M.–5 P.M. Off-season, tours
are offered at 11 A.M. and 2 and 5 P.M.

Wheelchairs accommodated? Yes.

Tastings

Charge for tasting with tour? $4.50, or
in tastings of two wines for $6 or three
wines for $9. Also, appetizers available
at the tasting salon.
Charge for tasting without tour?
As above.

Typical wines offered: Sparkling: Brut,
Blanc de Noirs, Extra-Dry Reserve, and
Rosé; still: Chardonnay, Pinot Noir, and
Pinot Meunier.

Sales of wine-related items? Yes.

Picnics and Programs

Picnic area open to the public? No
(restaurant on property).

Special events or wine-related
programs? Private Cellar Wine Club,
email newsletter. Special events
throughout the year; check website.

The marriage of past and present in a Napa Valley winery is best demonstrated at Domaine Chandon, on the western side of Yountville, with its sparkling-wine facility and restaurant. It seems appropriate that this town, named for George C. Yount, who planted the first Napa Valley grape rootstock in 1838, would be home to another innovation—the first French-owned California winery.

Moët-Hennessey–Louis Vuitton is today's name for the massive French holding company that took a chance in 1973 and purchased vineyard land in three Napa Valley areas—Yountville, the Mount Veeder hills, and Carneros. The goal of the company and master winemaker Edmund Maudière was to grow Chardonnay, Pinot Noir, and Pinot Meunier grapes for sparkling-wine production. Simultaneously, the company decided to open a restaurant of high caliber where the sparkling wines, as well as Napa Valley still wines, would be presented in an ideal setting for food and wine. None of the dedication to excellence has decreased at the stone-and-cement contemporary-style hospitality center and winery since its 1977 opening.

Near the landscaped entry road, an abstract fountain plays in one of the man-made ponds. Across the wooden footbridge is an underground hub of tourist activity. There you will find a visual display on various sizes of Champagne bottles. Some visitors walk up the interior cement steps and head for the restaurant; others choose to go directly to the salon at the head of the stairs, where they can sit at tables and purchase sparkling wine and appetizers. The majority of tourists congregate downstairs for the half-hour walking tour of the winery. Although the Grand Central Station–level noise tends to mask the tour guide's opening remarks, the basic elements of the tour are friendly, educational, and performed with style. Tour groups are large here—thirty to forty visitors—but the guides have an unintimidating manner that invites questions from novices and experts. Photography is encouraged. Expect a good number of steps on this tour, as the facilities are built on different levels.

There is a thrill similar to discovering a secret in walking the area lined with rows of fourteen-thousand-gallon stainless-steel fermentation tanks. Eloquent guides such as Bill Thomas describe the *méthode champenoise* procedure of in-bottle fermentation, and they are assisted by clear graphics, which demonstrate the movement of the dead yeast sediment. This yeast collects in the bottle and then is manipulated by riddling down into the bottle's neck for easy removal. In the riddling area, to which you descend, two hundred thousand bottles of wine rest their necks in wooden riddling racks, waiting silently for daily quarter-turns.

Within the Napa Valley, there is some confusion concerning the naming of sparkling wines. Some wineries call it Champagne; others dub it Napa Valley Champagne; and "sparkling wine" is used by many. Actually, all forms of nomenclature are legally correct. The Treaty of Madrid stated that only sparkling wine from the Champagne region of France could be called "Champagne." European countries signed the agreement in 1890, and, as a result, Spain calls its sparkling wine *cava*, Italy calls it *spumanti*, and Germany names it *secht*. However, the United States never

that large beads are called toad's eyes and that she believes there is some truth to the tale, although it has not been proven. She is quick to point out that the froth of bubbles atop a freshly poured glass of sparkling wine is called a mousse and not a head. "That's another beverage," she states with a smile.

Back upstairs you'll view the entire final wine-processing system from an upper platform. The stages of activity are well marked, so that the process is clear, even from the noisy peak of disgorging, corking, and bottle-tumbling to the final foiling, labeling, and box-ing of the bottles.

Given a dormant bottling line, the tour guide will use the quiet platform area to demonstrate how to properly open a bottle of sparkling wine. Basic information is given, such as "Chill it three hours in the refrigerator or at least forty minutes in an ice bucket," as well as sparkling-wine trivia: the speed at which a cork exits the bottle (sixty-two miles per hour) and how many counterclockwise turns will release the wire cage on any sparkling-wine bottle in the world (six and one-half).

Good-byes are said alongside the Beaujolais horizontal-style press, which was used from 1600 through the late 1800s. The press is mounted near an imposing modern stone arch.

Without question, this winery blends the old and the new with strong touches of education and hospitality.

signed, on the principle that our "don't tread on me" attitude should not yield to such a dictate from Europe. Also, the later experience of Prohibition made the concept of sparkling wine produced in this country unthinkable. In any case, Domaine Chandon defers to the treaty's ruling because of the company's French parentage. Ergo, this sparkling wine is called just that.

To keep up with the high-volume production of Domaine Chandon's Brut, Blanc de Noirs, Reserve, Première, Etoile, and Vintage sparkling styles, very large machines (amusingly called VLMs) riddle hun-dreds of bottles simultaneously, creating the same small beads (bubbles) as the hand-riddled wine.

"Is it true," asks a tourist, "that the larger the bubbles, the larger the headache?" The guide responds

Frog's Leap Winery
8815 Conn Creek Road
Rutherford, CA 94573
(707) 963-4704 or (800) 959-4704
fax (707) 963-0242
Website: www.frogsleap.com
Email: ribbit@frogsleap.com

Hours open for visits and tastings:
9 A.M.–5 P.M. Monday through Saturday.
Closed Sunday.

Winemaker: John Williams
Winery owner: John Williams

Access
Location: Going north on Highway 29
to Rutherford, turn right at Rutherford
Road. As the road descends, veer to
the left and look for the red barn with
the frog weathervane.

Appointment necessary for tour? Yes.

Wheelchairs accommodated? Yes.

Tastings
Charge for tasting with tour? No fee
for tour, but the tour must be reserved
ahead of time; maximum, twelve
guests.
Charge for tasting without tour? No,
but by appointment only.

Typical wines offered: Sauvignon Blanc,
Chardonnay, Leapfrögmilch, Zinfandel,
Merlot, Cabernet Sauvignon, and
Rutherford.

Sales of wine-related items? Yes.

Picnics and Programs
Picnic area open to the public? No.

Special events or wine-related
programs? No.

FROG'S LEAP WINERY

A sincere commitment to fun is one of the key elements of the Frog's Leap Winery mission, as is the 130-acre winery's dedication to the land. Taking a tour here is a must if you're ready to kick back, relax, and enjoy the whole exuberant process. Word has spread about this fun-loving place, so expect to share your visit with wine lovers from all over the world.

Your guided tour, limited to small numbers and very personal in style, starts at a picnic table outside the tasting room, a cottagelike building to the right of an actual frog pond. While seated around the table, you'll have a view of both the Mayacamas and the Vaca mountain ranges that edge Napa Valley. Note that the Mayacamas Range, where an average eighty inches of rain fall annually, is dense with trees and tall plants year-round; on the other hand, the Vaca Range might receive twenty-four inches of precipitation, yielding barren hills throughout the year. The visitor group tastes the first wine of the walk-around tour and then, with a glass of Sauvignon Blanc in hand, steps into the vineyards.

The vineyard discussion opens with organic vineyard practices—no chemicals are used here, as owner/winemaker John Williams sees the organic wine-making process as a "partnership with the fruit."

In season, cover crops line the earthy corridors between rows of vines: winter peas, crimson cloves, and some legumes add their verdant touches to the soil. Owl and raptor perches stand tall in the thirty-nine acres planted to Merlot surrounding the winery buildings; birds of prey station themselves at the ready to swoop down on rabbits and other vineyard creatures that nibble new vine shoots. Here, dry farming stresses the roots in a positive manner similar to some French vineyard practices. This practice of leaving the roots to exist on their own is unlike that seen in many Napa Valley vineyards, where a drip system is used to irrigate the vines. "We want to leave the land better than we found it," says the tour guide, Ann, who sees herself as a steward of this land.

Then you'll walk through the fruit-flower-vegetable garden, tossing excess wine onto the lawn as you amble to the eighteen-thousand-square-foot barrel chai (pronounced "shay"), crafted of recycled hundred-year-old Canadian timber. The chai houses three thousand barrels, stacked four barrels high, below and above ground level. Just across the gravelly path, now with Merlot in your glass, you'll visit the original barn, built in 1884, with its distinctive weathervane in the shape of a leaping frog. Expect to see dimpled, square, stainless-steel fermenting tanks made in Germany and able to hold one-third more wine than standard round tanks do. And you'll learn the serendipitous story of how John Williams entered Napa Valley wine making in the first place. Also, you'll view the stunning valley vineyards from an upper barn window, enjoy some Cabernet Sauvignon, and shoot hoops. Right! The end of the tour is the Frog's Leap Challenge: shoot a basketball through the (rather askew) hoop inside the barn. But then, such whimsy could be expected from a winery known for its fruit-forward wines and its motto: "Time's fun when you're having flies."

GRGICH HILLS CELLAR

Grgich Hills Cellar
1829 St. Helena Highway
Rutherford, CA 94573
(800) 532-3057
fax (707) 963-8725
Website: www.grgich.com
Email: info@grgich.com

Winemaker: Miljenko "Mike" Grgich
Winery owners: Miljenko "Mike" Grgich
and Austin Hills

Access
Location: On Highway 29, a half-mile
north of Rutherford, on the west side
of the highway.

Hours open for visits and tastings:
9:30 A.M.–4:30 P.M. daily, except New
Year's Day, Easter, Good Friday (half
day), Thanksgiving, and Christmas.

Appointment necessary for tour? Yes.
Tours at 11 A.M. and either 1:30 or
2 P.M., depending on the date.

Wheelchairs accommodated? Yes.

Tastings
Charge for tasting with tour? $5 per
glass, including a souvenir Grgich
Hills glass.
Charge for tasting without tour?
As above.

Typical wines offered: Chardonnay,
Fumé Blanc, Merlot, Zinfandel,
Cabernet Sauvignon, and late-harvest
Violetta (a dessert wine).

Sales of wine-related items? Yes.

Picnics and Programs
Picnic area open to the public? No.

Special events or wine-related
programs? Miljenko's Cellar Club
and the Pre-Release Club, which
entitles members to early notification
of new wines.

At a time when U.S. wine marketing is based generally on wine with food, Miljenko "Mike" Grgich is a man whose winery is doing something specific about it.

The tour at Grgich Hills Cellar begins and ends with discussion of the link between wine making and food preparation, with specific examples showing the similarities. Take chicken stock. At home, you can make a delicious stock by combining essential base ingredients—at least chicken, onion, carrots, celery, and salt—in a pot with water, bringing it to a boil, and then letting the rich flavors steep into the liquid during a slow simmer. You skim fats and residues that float to the surface, or, for further refining, you can stir foamy egg whites into the broth as a "food magnet" to attract and hold tiny food particles. A fine sieve can then remove those impurities.

While standing in the award-bedecked tasting room, the knowledgeable Grgich guide explains how wine making is a similar series of activities. By combining flavor bases—grapes from various vineyards picked at different times and temperatures—and allowing the grapes to sit together, you induce fermentation, and a cap of residue forms. The cap is then strained off and the fermented grape juice is refined, often with the help of egg whites, and bottled as wine, one of the few living, breathing, fermenting beverages.

"Wine is a living thing," the tour guide explains. "It will change over time because it is alive. Not so for spirits, which will never change."

The tour moves from the overly dark tasting room into the day's brilliance back at the winery's entry, and on to the edge of one of the early Grgich Hills vineyards paralleling Highway 29. There you'll learn that all the grapes are picked by hand, a dictate from Mike Grgich. Grgich is also the winemaker, hav-

ing immigrated from Croatia with a strong desire to make wine; Austin Hills, the winery's co-owner, is an heir to the Hills Brothers coffee fortune. Hills jumped at the chance of partnership with Grgich immediately after the 1976 Paris "crowning" of the '73 Chateau Montelena Chardonnay, when he was winemaker there. Grgich had taken enology studies at the University of Zagreb and still wears a student beret.

As a winery to visit, Grgich Hills is ideal for connoisseurs and for those who wish to learn about wine making. You'll learn such tips as how to differentiate American oak barrels from French ones (American barrels have a narrow belly compared to the French, which can hold as much as 3.3 gallons more wine).

Why use oak barrels? The guide explains that there's a biochemical interchange of phenol from the oak into the aging wine, which adds more flavor to the final product.

During a walk through the wine-making facility, you may see a number of cold-stabilization tanks jacketed in ice. Grgich, who follows classic wine-making techniques, filters his wines using this increasingly popular method of refining the fermented juice. Racking is another preferred technique that removes the depleted yeast and grape solids gently, resulting in a more "natural" wine. The wine tasting conducted for the tour sometimes takes place inside, but on a sunny day, you'll sit outside in leafy shade under the trees or the redwood trellis. Only the hum of traffic on Highway 29 will distract you as you and the other guests in your group sip Napa Valley Chardonnay, late-harvest Violetta, and other varietals while learning how to taste wine and compare vintages.

You might see Mike Grgich as you travel around the winery—watch for the man in a beret. If he is able to put his projects on hold, he'll happily answer your wine-making questions, adding to the wealth of understanding you will have gained from the tour.

THE HESS COLLECTION WINERY

The Hess Collection Winery
4411 Redwood Road
Napa, CA 94558
(707) 255-1144
fax (707) 253-1682
Website: www.hesscollection.com
Email: info@hesscollection.com

Winemaker: Dave Guffy
Winery founder: Donald Hess

Access
Location: Going north on Highway 29 to the town of Napa, stay in the left-hand lane; turn left on Redwood Road at its intersection with Trancas. Continue west about 6 miles to the winery.

Hours open for visits and tastings: 10 A.M.–4 P.M. daily, except New Year's Day, Easter, Thanksgiving, and Christmas.

Appointment necessary for tour? No; all tours are self-guided.

Wheelchairs accommodated? Yes.

Tastings
Charge for tasting with tour? $3, not deductible from price of purchased wine. No charge to view art galleries. Charge for tasting without tour? As above.

Typical wines offered: Current releases of Chardonnay and Cabernet Sauvignon.

Sales of wine-related items? Yes, including museum catalog.

Picnics and Programs
Picnic area open to the public? No.

Special events or wine-related programs? Creative food and wine pairings offered every Friday; included in tasting fee. Also, private dinners can be arranged; call ext. 226 for the events coordinator.

Redwood Road winds along the southwestern hills of Napa, leading you through shaded forests of sequoias and fields of mountain wildflowers. Solitary hawks glide effortlessly, dotting clear blue skies with their graceful forms. There is a subtle similarity here to driving circuitous routes in the Sierra foothills. Without question, this road is Northern California at its best.

With such a dramatic approach as Redwood Road leading to the Hess Collection Winery and museum, you might predict a lesser experience at road's end. But the truth is that the adventure only continues.

Walking from the parking area to the winery, you'll pass a sculpture garden and then face two splendid stone structures, merged by an internal spine of clean, contemporary architecture. The main building was constructed around 1903 as Mount La Salle, home for Northern California Christian Brothers. Once inside, you'll experience airy spaciousness. There is a mix of early-twentieth-century stonework and quiet modern lines that acts as a background for art and a stage for winery procedures.

The gratis tour here is self-guided and incorporates elements of the art of wine making with a museum of contemporary paintings and sculptures that are mounted in a thirteen-thousand-square-foot gallery. Visitors have the opportunity to view works by Frank Stella, Magdalena Abakanowicz, Francis Bacon, and other world-renowned artists. This museum is winery founder Donald Hess's "gift to the public." Hess is a Swiss-American ninth-generation brewmaster based in Bern. There he headquarters a variety of companies including an alpine trout hatchery and eighteen restaurants.

Hess believed that his vineyards, winery, and museum would fare well on Mount Veeder, an extinct volcano in the Mayacamas Range, due to the stress of surviving in the rocky soil of the Mount Veeder appellation. He had good reason. Although a visit to the hilly vineyards is not possible, they can be viewed in two ways: stop at one of the gallery's dormer windows and glance at the promontory across the way. You may see workers pruning the vines. Or take a few minutes to view the nine-projector slide show in the small theater on the winery's second floor. The seats are as comfortable as the plushest theater accommodation, and the room is a cool respite on a scorching day.

The slide presentation is the finest of any I have seen in the industry. The images take you through the 130-day push in the grape-growing cycle. Pictures and music highlight seasonal changes while they introduce

the people, techniques, and equipment necessary to make fine wine.

On exiting the theater, you can't miss Leopold Malers's *Hommage 1974*, a flaming typewriter that is a powerful image.

After the self-guided tour (with easy access by stairway or elevator), you will pass the massive floral arrangement on the first floor and proceed to the tast-ing room. There you'll find a huge wooden bar in a room surrounded by stone walls and aging barrels. The room's warm tones contrast with the gallery's brightness. The hosts and hostesses can answer any wine-making or tasting questions about the winery's Cabernet Sauvignons and Chardonnays.

My guess is that this winery visit will be one of the most memorable of your Napa Valley tour.

ROBERT MONDAVI WINERY

Robert Mondavi Winery
7801 St. Helena Highway
Oakville, CA 94562
(707) 963-9611 or (888) RMONDAVI
fax (707) 251-4386
Website: www.robertmondaviwinery.com
Email: info@robertmondaviwinery.com

Winemaker: Tim Mondavi
Winery owners: Robert Mondavi family

Access
Location: On Highway 29, one-eighth
mile north of Oakville.

Hours open for visits and tastings:
9 A.M.–6 P.M. daily, except New Year's
Day, Thanksgiving, and Christmas.

Appointment necessary for tour?
Recommended.

Wheelchairs accommodated? Yes.

Tastings
Charge for tasting with tour? Tours,
including tasting, start at $10.
Charge for tasting without tour? Yes;
prices vary according to wine and
vintage.

Typical wines offered: Chardonnay,
Sauvignon Blanc, Fumé Blanc,
Cabernet Sauvignon, and Pinot Noir.

Sales of wine-related items? Yes, in
retail store.

Picnics and Programs
Picnic area open to the public? No.

Special events or wine-related
programs? Many programs on wine,
wine making, and the history of food
and wine. Many programs include
luncheon in the Vineyard Room or in
the vineyard. Also, the Robert Mondavi
Summer Jazz Festival and the Great
Chefs Program, among others.

The entrance to the Robert Mondavi Winery in Oakville is a generous one, much like the spirit of its founder, who has tirelessly led the California wine industry since he founded his family company in 1966. Broad steps lead past a sleek granite bear sculpted by Beniamino Bufano, and as you approach the terrace the massive mission-style arch frames a splendid vista of the western vineyards and hills.

To many who make the pilgrimage to the valley, the Robert Mondavi Winery is Mecca, and their hopes of learning about wine are answered here at the winery known, above all others in the Napa Valley, for its excellent tours.

"Let me say that there are as many different wines as there are types of bread, or of fish in the sea," notes tour guide Kurt Cobbett as he leads a group of twenty-five guests from the visitors' center into the vineyard. With that opener, Kurt sets the two themes that are clearly elemental to the Robert Mondavi family philosophy: education leads to knowledge and enjoyment, and wine is a natural accompaniment to food.

If you tour during the late summer and at harvest time you'll be encouraged to sample some of the many varieties of grapes from the demonstration vineyard just beyond the arch, where some discussion on the history of wine will take place. For instance, wine has its roots in the Middle East, where wine vessels dating to 7000 B.C. have been discovered. It's no wonder that grapes thrive in the dry, desertlike climate of the Napa Valley, where rainfall is typically absent from April through November.

Moving from the vineyard to the new To Kalon Fermentation Cellar, completed in time for harvest 2000, guests learn that the stemmer-crusher, which looks like a giant cheese grater, is used to separate grapes from their stems before crushing them. Seemingly small details are added during the discussion, such as the tip that Pinot Noir stems are allowed to remain with the grapes, whereas Cabernet Sauvignon stems are removed. If you took notes during a Robert Mondavi tour, you could almost go home and make your own vintage; there are no secrets here.

Once inside the vast cellar lined with fifty-six huge French oak fermentation tanks—each holding five thousand gallons—the guide explains fermentation as "nothing more than little yeast cells eating grape juice."

"How can a red grape give white wine?" asks one tourist. I've heard Kurt, as well as other Robert Mondavi tour guides, answer by referring to a differ-

ent fruit: "Think of an apple. It has red skin, white fruit, and clear juice, just like a grape. If we want white wine, we squeeze the juice and remove the skins. If we want to make red wine, we leave the skins in with the juice for a certain amount of time and then press the mixture and strain off the skins."

Due to the simplified explanations of the ancient art of wine making, you can finally understand the basic process, and you'll see other heads nodding as you walk to the Barrel Cellar. The tour guide continues to demystify wine making while reviewing serious numbers such as the cost of French oak barrels, around six hundred dollars each.

One of the tour's most pleasant walks follows the visit to the technical wine-making wing of the operation. Tourists stroll around the renowned To Kalon vineyard bordered by rosebushes. The To Kalon renovation project resulted in a new state-of-the-art facility for producing and barrel-aging the winery's high-end reds as well as improvements to the winery visitors' programs.

The extensive manicured lawn at Robert Mondavi stretches toward the entry; this lawn is the scene of summer-evening jazz concerts, during which the winery has presented such greats as Ella Fitzgerald and Ray Charles, while visitors picnic on the green.

Following the terra-cotta tiles along the lawn's curve, you'll pass the Vineyard Room off the hospitality wing. There the Mondavi family, under the guidance of Margrit Biever (Robert Mondavi's wife), hosts art shows, concerts, and literary presentations in conjunction with its mission to link wine appreciation with recognition of all the arts. It is the same dedication to the merging of the worlds of wine, food and the arts that led Robert and Margrit to inspire COPIA, the center founded in 2001 at the "oxbow" of the Napa River in the city of Napa.

Your group will conclude its tour with an extensive tasting, which once again promotes education along with enjoyment. You will settle in one of the new private tasting rooms or in a shaded area outside. The Mondavi tour guides share a word to the wise about wine tasting: "Just pretend you're eating a hamburger—look at it, smell it, and taste it. It's that simple."

During the tasting, questions and observations are encouraged. When a question is posed on the relation of the color of red wine to vintage, the guide places a white linen napkin over a plate and pours a bit of '79 Cabernet Reserve on it, beside an '82 and an '87, to discuss the differences. Aging causes a slightly brown tinge due to oxidation, which shows

on the napkin. Younger wines usually yield a more intense color.

With its vigorous dedication to the marriage of food with wine, the winery has a full complement of chefs who prepare meals for special events. At this writing, Mondavi is one of the few wineries that offer a taste of food other than crackers or bread to complement a tour's wine tasting. As an example, small squares of a peach tart—and its recipe—are offered in tandem with Moscato d'Oro dessert wine.

The educational-tour-and-taste program was initiated at the opening of the Robert Mondavi Winery, at a time when there were only twenty-six active wineries in the Napa Valley. Since then, nearly four hundred wineries have grown along Highway 29 and the Silverado Trail as well as on the western and eastern slopes. Throughout all the expansion, this winery has been a central beacon to visitors, growers, and vintners.

MUMM NAPA ESTATES

Mumm Napa Estates
8445 Silverado Trail
Rutherford, CA 94573
(707) 967-7700
fax (707) 967-7796
Website: www.mummcuveenapa.com
Email: mumm_info@mummcuveenapa.com

Winemaker: Ludovic Dervin
Winery owner: Allied Domecq Wines

Access
Location: Five minutes' drive south
of St. Helena on the Silverado Trail,
between Conn Creek Road (Highway
128) and Oakville Cross Road.

Hours open for visits and tastings:
10 A.M.–5 P.M.

Appointment necessary for tour?
No. Complimentary tours hourly,
10 A.M.–3 P.M.

Wheelchairs accommodated? Yes.

Tastings
Charge for tasting with tour? $3.75
or more per flute (full glass), not
deductible from price of purchased
wine.
Charge for tasting without tour?
As above.

Typical wines offered: Brut Prestige,
Blanc de Noirs, Blanc de Blancs,
and DUX.

Sales of wine-related items? Yes;
many logo and wine-related items.

Picnics and Programs
Picnic area open to the public? No.

Special events or wine-related
programs? Two fine-art photography
collections, including "Private
Collection" by Ansel Adams.

A California plantation house. While you sit on the veranda at Mumm Napa Estates, sipping sparkling Blanc de Noirs and gazing westward over acres of Cabernet Sauvignon grapes, the image develops of a California-variety plantation. New Age flute music, white chairs, and creamy white Italian canvas umbrellas shading you from the sun's rays contrast with thriving green philodendron plants and verdigrised metal chairs in the glass-enclosed exteriors of the hospitality center. Massive *Casablanca*-style fans push soft breezes in the room while a young woman smiles and asks, "Sparkling wine or mineral water?"

This winery offers the California dream in contemporary style. Its facilities reveal wine-making equipment ranked among the most modern in the world.

Touring is easily done, all on one level, due to an excellent walkway system bordering the huge fermentation tanks. On autumn tours I have taken, the tour guides have been articulate, aware of the stages of the wine-making art, and sophisticated enough to relate to visitors from a variety of backgrounds. Three very short videos are presented during different points in the tour to demonstrate activities that occur only seasonally: the harvesting process, bottling, and disgorgement. In fact, in my opinion none of the tours and tour guides covered in this collection can rival those of Mumm Napa Estates, along with Robert Mondavi and St. Supéry, for comprehensive, visitor-friendly tours.

Your tour will depart from the visitors' center and proceed down a paved path to a minivineyard where Pinot Meunier, Chardonnay, Pinot Gris, and Pinot Noir grapes grow. Since the fruit used for actual production is grown "down valley" in the Carneros region, the small vineyard offers a practical demonstration of a year's cycle of grape growth.

The tour guide is sure to mention that "although all Champagne is sparkling wine, not all sparkling wines are Champagne." Almost every guide at every sparkling winery makes the same statement.

There is little discussion as you pass the fermentation tanks arranged as neatly as steel tanks in the most modern dairy. The largest tank of all is centrally located in the vast room. Its sixty-five-thousand-gallon capacity is described in a one-bottle measure: if you drank one standard-size (750-milliliter) bottle of wine a day, it would take 898 years to empty the vat.

At the walkway's end is an observation platform from which you'll see the arrival area for grapes during harvest. If you visit this or any winery during "the crush," as grape harvest is called, you'll see action. Workers are laboring six, sometimes seven days a week, twelve to fourteen hours per day. The fruit is delivered in bins as yellow as mustard on a hot dog.

Winemaker Ludovic Dervin has chosen the classic method of treating grapes for sparkling wines: the stemmer-crusher is employed because it is gentle on the grape skins. Rough handling would break the skins, releasing highly tannic seeds into the grape juice. "You want tannins in still wines," explains the tour guide, "but not in sparklers." When the just-crushed juice is siphoned into a tank, yeast is added immediately to help convert the juice's sugar into alcohol. This first fermentation method is identical to that of a still wine.

The difference in making sparkling wine in the *méthode champenoise* manner is that the wine is then funneled into heavy bottles, which are stopped with a small plastic *bidule* (translates from French as "thinga-majig"), which acts as a plug. The bottles are then capped with a metal soda-pop top. During the one and a half to four years the bottles lie on their sides, ninety to a hundred pounds of pressure per square inch build within each bottle. That's the same pressure as that inside a car tire, applied to a wine bottle.

By now, you are in a wide corridor looking through windows at a variety of activities: to one side is the automatic riddling room where VLMs (very large machines) are stacked with pallets of filled bottles. The VLMs turn every six hours to encourage the sedimentary mass of dead yeast cells to collect at the bottle necks. On the other side of the corridor, you'll see the impeccable large laboratory.

Look through yet another large window to view the freezing and disgorging treatments of the wine. Here, necks of bottles filled with aged, bottle-fermented wine are frozen automatically in a propylene glycol bath at negative twenty-three degrees centigrade, followed by removal of the metal caps. This action forces the *bidules* and frozen plugs of yeast to burst from the bottles. The *dosage*—addition of a small amount of sugar—reduces acidity and "softens" the wine.

Finally, on to a viewing station above the bottling line, where a hundred thousand cases of sparkling wine annually receive their corks, wire cages over the

corks, labels, and neck foils. The whole procedure is fully automated and moves with the precision of dancing figures in a music box.

There is a wall-mounted demonstration of how champagne corks are made, with layers of glued cork pressed into a mass that is then cut. The tour guide will field questions with ease, and will act as your waiter on returning to the visitors' center. There, for a charge, you can enjoy generous tastings of the various sparkling wines as well as sweet or savory appetizers while being shaded by the Italian umbrellas and lulled by the strains of flute music.

California indeed.

Niebaum-Coppola Estate Winery
1991 St. Helena Highway
Rutherford, CA 94573
(707) 968-1100 or (800) RUBICON
fax (707) 967-9084
Website: www.niebaum-coppola.com
Email: info@niebaum-coppola.com

Winemaker: Scott McLeod
Winery owners: Francis Ford and
Eleanor Coppola

Access

Location: On Highway 29, north of
Oakville in the town of Rutherford; first
left (to the west) after Niebaum Lane.

Hours open for visits and tastings:
10 A.M.–5 P.M. Monday through Saturday
and 8 A.M.–2 P.M. Sunday, except New
Year's Day, Easter, Thanksgiving,
Christmas Eve, and Christmas Day.

Appointment necessary for tour? No.

Wheelchairs accommodated? Yes.

Tastings

Charge for tasting with tour? Yes;
prices vary for tastings. Two tours
are offered, each costing $20.
The historical chateau tour at
10:30 A.M., 12:30 P.M., and 2:30 P.M.;
the vineyard tour is at 11:00 A.M,
weather permitting.
Charge for tasting without tour?
As above.

Typical wines offered: Wines vary
depending on availability.

Sales of wine-related items? Yes.

Picnics and Programs

Picnic area open to the public? No.

Special events or wine-related
programs? Call for information
about special events: (707) 968-1100.

When you turn off Highway 29 onto the Rutherford property of the Niebaum-Coppola Estate Winery, imagine that you're bouncing in a horse-drawn carriage down the one-fifth-mile entry drive.

The earth to your right and left has yielded wine grapes since Finnish fur trader Captain Gustave Niebaum founded this winery in 1879. As you alight from your "carriage," you'll become aware of a deep sense of dual traditions here. Ivy-covered winery buildings face a square as large as the hub of some European towns. The original stone winery lies to the west of a massive reflecting pool. The ninety-foot-long pool was added as part of a major interior and exterior refurbishing of the property by Francis Ford and Eleanor Coppola, who have been, since late 1994, the owners of this historic winery chateau and vineyard land in the heart of the Napa Valley.

The wine-making facility is a reminder of late-nineteenth-century Bordeaux-style architecture. The particularly interesting mix here is the fact that renowned film director Coppola has put his stamp inside the stone chateau, with such additions as flashy *Dracula* costumes, plans from the filming of *Apocalypse Now*, and the desk from the original set of *The Godfather*, all of which are housed on the second floor of the building. The result? A mesh of old and new traditions, both bent on pleasing the public with memorable sights and wines.

By noting the building's fine details, you will understand why it was five years in construction, opening in 1879. To best appreciate the place, step over the original "Inglenook" embedded in the stone entry and walk around the entry hall to view the Captain's Room. More a museum than a hospitality center, the room resembles a ship's wardroom, down to its porthole window, shelf railings, and latched cupboard doors. The room and entry hall house a four-hundred-year-old glass lamp and sixteenth-century Flemish wine cups and other valuable items. From here, you will face the grand staircase enhanced by buttery wooden pedestals hand-carved from wood imported from Belize (where the Coppolas own a lavish resort).

To the right is a series of rooms including a well-stocked retail space, possibly the largest in a Napa Valley winery. Eleanor Coppola chooses most of the items, which range from pasta to home-grown olive oil to a variety of tableware, books, corkscrews, and more. Adjacent is the wine-tasting room. The winery pours numerous wine varietals, offering a chance to zero in on elegant vintages or wines for more relaxed dining. Two tours are offered, one emphasizing the historical side of the winery, the other a vineyard tour, each at twenty dollars per person.

Keep your eyes open as you walk upstairs and you'll spy an original Tucker (an auto featured in Coppola's film of the same name). Look to one side of

the automobile and you'll see five Oscars amassed by the Coppolas over the years. Behind the stairs, you'll see a glass-encased Niebaum, Inglenook, and Coppola memorabilia collection that evokes the inevitable sense of living with history, once again demonstrating the two sides of tradition awaiting the winery visitor.

Another find is the extensive wine library to the left of the main entrance. The bottle collection houses Inglenook vintages dating back to 1887. Although ancient vintages are not available for public tasting, they are occasionally offered for extraordinary auctions or wine-industry tastings.

During your stay at the winery, you will probably learn about the typical Napa Valley soil so important to the success of the wines. Ask any guide for information on the earth in this Rutherford region. You will find that it is rocky, well-drained, and alluvial. The first layer of soil typical in the Napa Valley, also called the top layer of "plowed pan," contains a mixture of dark humus and the blue-gray Bale clay. History states that when Captain Niebaum bought the property, he diverted the stream to the north, but the underlying sandy and gravelly sediments from the meandering stream remain, yielding alluvial soil. Sandstone gravels and highly colored chert pebbles eroded from the second and third layers. Chert, created as a result of high heat, proves past vol-

canic activity in the area. The fourth layer is an interface of cobbles incorporated with clay, and the base is bedrock. It is important to understand that poor, rocky soil requires roots to stretch and to hold it during their typical thirty-year life span.

An explanation of the soil sheds light on answers to two frequent questions concerning vineyard management:

How often do you water the vines? Rarely, if at all. Roots seek out the water level, which is twenty to thirty feet below the surface. However, vineyard managers often install a drip irrigation system to handle overly dry soil during times of drought and extreme heat.

Do you uproot the vines frequently? There are some vines here in the Napa Valley that have survived for well over fifty years. For example, Trefethen, Beringer, and Niebaum-Coppola are a few vineyards with some rootstock of that age or older. The vines still bear fruit. In the Napa Valley, rootstock remains planted thirty years on average, unless there is a plant disease.

Real wine-making history was made by Captain Niebaum's great-nephew, John Daniel, Jr., during the thirty years he headed Inglenook, from

1934 to 1964. Among other giant strides, Daniel promoted and gained acceptance for the Napa Valley appellation, pioneered vintage-dating of wines, and pushed for varietal designations for wines from the region, all steps toward solidifying the valley as a home of great wines.

What else is in store for the chateau? Francis Ford and Eleanor Coppola brought one of their dreams into reality by reinstating the wine-making facility on the second floor of the chateau with the opening of their Rubicon Winery in 2002. Cabernet had not been fermented here since the harvest of 1966 on the property. The Rubicon is certified organic, part of the wine-growing movement that is returning vines to their natural, nonchemically treated style of growth.

It is clear that the in-chateau winery is just the tip of Coppola's hopes for the future of the winery. Who knows what "Gustave's Godfather" will dream up next?

Joseph Phelps Vineyards
200 Taplin Road
St. Helena, CA 94574
(707) 963-2745
fax (707) 963-4831
Website: www.jpvwines.com
Email: jpvwines@aol.com

Winemaker: Craig Williams
Winery owners: Joseph Phelps,
chairman; Tom Shelton, C.E.O.

Access
Location: Driving north on the
Silverado Trail, one-half-mile north
of Zinfandel Lane, turn onto Taplin
Road—it's the first winery on the left.

Hours open for visits and tastings:
9 A.M.–5 P.M. Monday through Friday,
10 A.M.–5 P.M. Saturday, 10 A.M.–4 P.M.
Sunday, except major holidays.

Appointment necessary for tour? No
tours, but reservations recommended
for tastings and seminars.

Wheelchairs accommodated? Yes.

Tastings
Charge for tasting with tour? No tours.
Charge for tasting without tour? $15
for a 1½-hour seminar and tasting of
six to seven wines (reservations
recommended) at 11 A.M. and 2:30 P.M.
weekdays. Saturdays and Sundays,
1 hour seminar four times a day (call
for times); $5 for tasting of current
releases on the hour 10 A.M.–3 P.M.
daily.

Typical wines offered: Those currently
available—usually four—including
Cabernet Sauvignon and Chardonnay.

Sales of wine-related items? Yes.

Picnics and Programs
Picnic area open to the public? Yes,
though not always available; request
permission in advance.

Special events or wine-related
programs? No.

JOSEPH PHELPS VINEYARDS

The forest-green Spring Valley schoolhouse on Taplin Road along the Silverado Trail is a showstopper. The century-old school sits unchanged in a woodsy glen, marking the entrance to the Joseph Phelps Vineyards property, where you'll find one of the truly spectacular views in the valley, particularly in springtime. Drive up Taplin to the imposing gateway crafted from redwood bridge timbers. Once on Phelps's land, you may feel a sense of the Napa Valley as it was at the start of the twentieth century. The reason for this nostalgic vision is that Joe Phelps planted grape rootstock on only 175 acres of the former Connolly Hereford Ranch, thus maintaining rolling hills and erratic hillocks throughout 600 acres of prime land, much as it was when visits to neighboring ranches were by horse and buggy.

Phelps, who came to the valley with a background as a contractor, is typical of those who visited and decided to remain. During the late 1960s, he was hired to build two Souverain wineries, then owned by the Pillsbury Company. Today those wineries are Rutherford Hill in the Napa Valley and Chateau Souverain in the Alexander Valley. As a result of those experiences, he purchased this property for his own winery, which he built in a big-timber Colorado style. Massive redwood beams mesh with steel and glass,

giving a feeling of solid new tradition built to last the test of time.

If you arrive in the spring, masses of pale-violet wisteria will drape the redwood timbers that bridge the winery's two pavilions—one housing the steel fermentation tanks and some small oak tanks, and the other housing the barrels made of French oak for aging Cabernets, Chardonnays, and other wines. In this pavilion, you'll also find Yugoslavian oak used, because it does not impart flavors to Sauvignon Blancs and Gewürztraminers. The wisteria hints at the beautiful flower beds awaiting the visitor, particularly those beds viewed while looking down the vineyard from the back patio.

Each time I've visited Phelps Vineyards, two distinct characteristics of the visitors have manifested themselves: first, many guests are true flower fanciers and come to view the plantings, and, second, the tourists seem to be a fun-loving group. There is no explaining this latter enthusiastic spirit, unless it is the joie de vivre of the cheerful guides at the winery.

The seminar commences on the patio in fair weather, or in the guest center. There, visitors learn that this one winery produces twelve to fifteen different varietal wines with a bottling of only one hundred thousand cases, a relatively small production for most

wineries that have land holdings of four hundred acres (Phelps also owns vineyards in Oakville, Rutherford, Yountville, Stags Leap, and Carneros in the Napa Valley, as well as in King City in Monterey County).

Despite the quiet panorama from the patio, there is furious activity at the Taplin Road winery property and much for wine fanciers to learn. Phelps exemplifies the use of stainless steel for fermentation, and it was at this winery that the true Syrah grape of France's Rhône Valley was first bottled in California, as opposed to the state's more recognized Petite Syrah.

After visiting the 3,500 barrels in the cool fermentation chambers, a tasting under the patio arbor is perfectly timed. You'll taste at least four wines, perhaps more, depending on the seminar guide and the time of day. The shaded picnic area, which must be reserved ahead, is an ideal nook above the vineyards.

In fact, you could plan a complete Joseph Phelps–inspired outing: call ahead to reserve a tour and request a table at the Phelps picnic area, then shop at the Oakville Grocery on Highway 29 at Oakville Cross Road (the picnic-perfect grocery is one of Phelps's projects; it offers an array of cheeses, breads, wine, pastries, and international goodies). With your basket filled, head for "the Trail" and Taplin Road in time for your seminar and then settle down for a relaxed outdoor meal with wine from the source. Such a day, wrapped in memories of wisteria and wine, will long be remembered.

PRIDE MOUNTAIN VINEYARDS

Pride Mountain Vineyards
4026 Spring Mountain Road
St. Helena, CA 94574
(707) 963-4949
fax (707) 963-6039
Website: www.pridewines.com
Email: contactus@pridewines.com

Winemaker: Bob Foley
Winery founders: Jim and Carolyn
Pride

Access
Location: From the town of Napa, take
Highway 29 north to St. Helena and
turn left on Madrona. Take a right on
Spring Mountain Road and go 5.5 miles
to the ranch driveway, number 9175;
a sign at the bottom of the driveway
reads "Pride."

Hours open for visits and tastings:
Tours at 10 A.M. Wednesday through
Monday; tastings 10 A.M.–3:30 P.M.
Wednesday through Monday. Closed
Christmas and New Year's Eve. Space
limited on each day; please call ahead.

Appointment necessary for tour? Yes,
and also for tastings.

Wheelchairs accommodated? Yes.

Tastings
Charge for tasting with tour? No.
Call ahead for tour reservation.
Charge for tasting without tour? $5.

Typical wines offered: Chardonnay,
Viognier, Merlot, Cabernet Sauvignon,
and Cabernet Franc.

Sales of wine-related items? Yes.

Picnics and Programs
Picnic area open to the public? Open to
winery visitors, by appointment only.

Special events or wine-related
programs? Seasonal wine-release
parties for mailing-list customers.

You may have thought all roads to Napa Valley wineries were more or less straight along Highway 29 or the Silverado Trail. Think again. The twisty road from the base of St. Helena's Spring Mountain to Pride Mountain Vineyards at its very top could be an outstanding test course for sports cars. The road moves this way, then that, then curves around again, always taking in spectacular views of massive redwood trees, vineyards, and occasional panoramas over the small town below. "I survived the drive to Pride" is emblazoned on a T-shirt in the cozy shop area of the tasting room. Survived, indeed, and it's well worth the trip to this vineyard and winery at Summit Ranch on the crest of the Mayacamas mountain range.

On first arrival at this two-hundred-acre mountaintop vineyard and winery, you might mistake the property for a rustic resort. The tasting room sports stone floors and wooden beams, and the welcoming staff dress in Rocky Mountain casuals rather than the Napa Valley "dressy casuals" you'd expect on the valley floor. All this adds to the approachable, friendly atmosphere of the vineyard and winery.

Pride Mountain is one of the few Napa Valley wineries where you are offered wine on arrival. While you are standing at the rustic tasting bar, viewing the display of antique saws, yokes, and other farm implements of old, a staff member might note that seventy-five acres of the mountaintop are planted to Merlot, Cabernet Sauvignon, and Chardonnay grapes. Some of the fruit is among the last to be harvested in the valley each year, due to the vineyard's 2,100-foot elevation and the cool temperatures that slow grape maturation.

The Napa/Sonoma county line runs through the middle of Pride Mountain's crush pad, dividing the property's watershed. As the winery visit begins, you face the cave near the crush pad. Napa is to the left of the cave, Sonoma to the right. Despite the fact that the twenty-two-thousand-square-foot caves are new and the vineyards show slender young vines, this land has been home to grapes since 1869. At that time, alpine farmers arriving from Switzerland, Italy, and France headed straight to these hills. They drove

the fruit by oxcart to the valley floor, the trip taking a day and a half. When you realize that the road up the mountain was not paved until 1950, it is clear that the early wines from this area were the result of major dedication.

In the early years, the county line was seen as a way to increase county revenue. A little one-room schoolhouse, known as the Diamond Mountain School, was built on skids so that it could be moved from one county to the other, depending on which county had more taxpaying families with children attending the school.

Thirty-five title changes have taken place over the life of this property. Since the Gamble family of Procter & Gamble owned the property until 1950, title has passed through several well-known wineries: Cuvaison, Larkmead, Robert Mondavi, and Philip Togni. Jim and Carolyn Pride bought the land in 1990; native Californians, they were born into farming families. Jim is the founder of Pride Institute, a consulting and management firm for dentists, but it was his ownership of an architectural and construction company that proved invaluable in building the new winery.

Be sure to wear rubber-soled shoes on this tour; it's a working winery. In the caves, you'll see French oak barrels used for red wines, American oak for whites; the 2000 barrels are racked no more than two barrels high. Watch for the zipperlike drains along the cave floor and the Bordeaux-style metal candleholders clamped onto barrels along the path to the dining chamber.

Another reason for comfortable shoes relates to the possibility that Corky and Rock, two Belgian draft horses from Missouri, each weighing a ton, may arrive hauling a covered wagon with seats for a close-up tour of the vineyards. With the vineyard manager guiding, the workhorses clop along dirt paths at a relaxed pace while you experience the grapes from a long arm's distance and view the Vaca Mountains across the valley. This is surely one of the most picturesque winery tours in the Napa Valley, including the picnic spot along the way. On return to the tasting room, the guide will pour a few more wine tastes during a final vintage discussion before you drive the twisting road to the valley floor.

RUTHERFORD HILL WINERY

Rutherford Hill Winery
200 Rutherford Hill Road
Rutherford, CA 94573
(707) 963-1871
fax (707) 963-1878
Website: www.rutherfordhill.com
Email: info@rutherfordhill.com

Winemaker: Dave Dobson
Winery owners: Terlato family of
the Terlato Wine Group (TWG)

Access

Location: On the Silverado Trail, just
north of the Rutherford Cross Road,
turn left onto Rutherford Hill Road.
(Look for the large inscribed rock.)

Hours open for visits and tastings:
10 A.M.–5 P.M. daily, except New
Year's Day, Easter, Thanksgiving,
and Christmas.

Appointment necessary for tour?
No—first come, first serve; limited
to thirty people per tour. Tours at
11:30 A.M. and 1:30 and 3:30 P.M.

Wheelchairs accommodated? Yes.

Tastings

Charge for tasting with tour? Tours
cost an additional $5 on top of tasting.
Charge for tasting without tour? $5 for
five wines and a logo glass; $10 for five
reserve wines and a reserve logo glass.

Typical wines offered: Chardonnay,
Sauvignon Blanc, Gewürztraminer,
Merlot, Cabernet Sauvignon, and
Zinfandel Port.

Sales of wine-related items? Yes.

Picnics and Programs

Picnic area open to the public? No.

Special events or wine-related
programs? Cave dining and wine-
blending sessions.

Spelunkers, take notice: there are forty-four-thousand square feet of caves in the eastern Napa Valley foothills above Rutherford Hill Winery. The cave system, which is 120 feet below ground in some areas, is one of the largest created for wine aging in North America. It was dug mechanically under the direction of Alf Bertleson during the 1980s and is secured with a gunite surface.

So, what does an extensive cave system have to do with Rutherford Hill wine, or any wine, for that matter? The use of caves for wine storage is an ancient tradition. The French word for cellar is *cave*, and we English-speakers have adopted the word to mean a cavern or hollowed-out chamber of earth. Historically, wines have been aged in caves because the temperature within the earth is often as low as or lower than the fifty-eight to sixty-two degrees ideal for barrel-aging. Also, the humidity within these caves is a constant 90 percent, reducing worry of wine evaporation through barrel pores.

For walking through the labyrinthine caves, consider wearing rubber-soled shoes. With such a high humidity level, the cement floors, which are continuously hosed for sanitary purposes, occasionally hold small pools of water, so sandals or high heels are bound to be uncomfortable. (A note on high heels in general for touring wineries: leave them in your car. They'll only slow you on gravel, in the fields, and in caves such as these.)

Rutherford Hill Winery grew from the successes of Freemark Abbey Winery. In 1976, Freemark Abbey co-owners Chuck Carpy, Bill Jaeger, and Laurie Wood decided to expand their operation by purchasing the former Souverain of Rutherford winery, which had been built in the early 1970s by Joseph Phelps. Later owners were the Pillsbury Mills company and the Bill Jaeger family. Then, in 1996, wine importer Anthony Terlato, with sons Bill and John, purchased the winery; they continue to focus its efforts on producing quality Merlot. This medium-sized winery now produces a hundred thousand cases a year.

Driving to the winery, you'll journey up the hill that also leads to Auberge du Soleil, an elegant resort built Riviera-style along the hill's face. Both the

resort and this winery at the crest offer a picturesque view of the land grant given by pioneer George Yount to his granddaughter in the mid-1800s on the occasion of her marriage to Thomas Rutherford.

The forty-minute tour often opens with an invitation to picnic under the shady oaks bordering a hundred-year-old olive grove. A friendly, open spirit is maintained throughout the tour as you walk from the massive, barn-style hospitality center and winery up a slight incline to view the spectacular panorama, and then into the cave system. Barrels are stacked four per pallet.

"Each barrel holds about sixty gallons of wine," notes the tour guide. "That's twenty-four cases per barrel." You can almost hear mental calculators whirring as tourists walk past cave after cave of neatly arranged French barrels. Interestingly, the barrels at Rutherford Hill arrive as precut staves, which are then assembled in the Napa Valley by coopers at Demptos Cooperage. The barrel wood composition is 75 percent French oak—drawn from twelve different varieties of oak—and 25 per cent American oak. "We find it advantageous to construct and repair the barrels in our own backyard," the guide explains. The caves hold eight thousand barrels.

After touring a number of wineries, it becomes commonplace to see bungs of varying construction. A bung is a wine barrel closure, and some are made of wood, some of plastic or silicone (as at Rutherford Hill), some of glass, and yet others of earthenware. Sometimes, you'll even see paper cups used at transition times, when barrels are empty for the moment, awaiting washing or new wine.

If you are lucky enough to be led by a tour guide with a resonant voice, be prepared for a pleasant earful as the sound reverberates.

From the caves, the tour moves through the area of ninety stainless-steel tanks, their dimpled encasements gleaming in the light. You will learn about various styles of filtration to clarify the wine for eventual bottling, including a state-of-the-art rotary fermenter.

Back at the visitors' center, you will be offered tastes of five wines. And if you are bound to shop, the retail room at Rutherford Hill offers items from wine chillers to crystal stemware to wine and food books to extra-virgin olive oil and balsamic vinegar.

Whether your fascination is with caves, wine making, or viewing a splendid panorama, Rutherford Hill can provide multiple diversions.

ST. CLEMENT VINEYARDS

St. Clement Vineyards
2867 St. Helena Highway North
St. Helena, CA 94574
(707) 967-3033 or (707) 963-7221
fax (707) 963-1412
Website: www.stclement.com
Email: info@stclement.com

Winemaker: Aaron Pott
Winery owner: Beringer Blass Wine
Estates

Access
Location: Just north of Deer Park Road
on the southwest side of Highway 29.

Hours open for visits and tastings:
10 A.M.–4 P.M. daily, except New Year's
Day, Easter, Thanksgiving, and
Christmas.

Appointment necessary for tour? Yes.
One tour at 10:30 A.M. daily.

Wheelchairs accommodated? Yes.

Tastings
Charge for tasting with tour? No.
Charge for tasting without tour? $5 for
five wines; $10 for reds only and wine
library vintages.

Typical wines offered: Sauvignon Blanc,
Chardonnay, Merlot, and Cabernet
Sauvignon, as well as limited-
production wines available only at
winery.

Sales of wine-related items? Yes,
including logo glasses ($5) and shirts.

Picnics and Programs
Picnic area open to the public? Yes,
by appointment only.

Special events or wine-related
programs? "Friends of St. Clement"
are sent a newsletter with news of
pre-releases and invited to attend
the annual Christmas Harvest Festival
and Christmas Open Houses.

Immediately following harvest, leaves on the Chinese pistachio trees splash a vibrant red-orange line along the south side of St. Clement Vineyards. This brilliant color contrasts dramatically with subtle gray-green wood siding and white trim on the Victorian home that crowns this western hillside vineyard just up the road from the Charles Krug Winery. Actually, the color of flames is symbolic of the phoenixlike existence that this small gem of a winery has known since it was built in 1876.

Fritz Rosenbaum, a San Francisco glass merchant who wished to join the estate vineyard boom in the Napa Valley, bought this property and constructed the tasteful home atop a small stone winery. The cellar was bonded in 1879, the eighth in the valley. Rosenbaum took great pride in producing his own wine, which he bottled under the name of Johanaberg Vineyards.

During and after Prohibition the winery fell into disrepair, until Michael Robbins, a real estate executive and wine connoisseur, bought the land in 1962 and renamed it Spring Mountain Vineyards. Robbins took meticulous care in renovating the house, where he lived until he sold it to Dr. William Casey in 1975. At that point, Robbins moved to Tiburcio Parrot's Miravalle estate on Spring Mountain Road, taking with him the Spring Mountain Vineyards name and label.

Once again the elegant little Victorian on the hill took on a new name. Casey named it St. Clement Vineyards, after the small Chesapeake Bay home island of his Maryland family and also in honor of the patron saint of mariners.

Winemaker Chuck Ortman, who had made wines in the same cellars for Mike Robbins's Spring Mountain wines, created the early vintages of Sauvignon Blanc, Chardonnay, and Cabernet Sauvignon under the new label. Dennis Johns, formerly at Sterling Vineyards, was St. Clement's winemaker for twenty years, and the position is now held by Aaron Pott. He oversees an annual production of twenty thousand cases of wine, making this one of the smaller wineries in the valley.

Sapporo USA, a Japanese brewing and winemaking company seeking to diversify its interests, next purchased Fritz Rosenbaum's Victorian home and cellar in 1987. Under the new proprietors, the winery home finally opened its doors to the public, with daily tastings and tours. This was the first Japanese group to invest in a Napa Valley winery; the number of such investments has now increased to four. In its most recent metamorphosis, the winery was purchased by

Beringer Blass Wine Estates in 1999, with the plan to leave the winery basically untouched.

Climb up the hill from the lower parking area, passing neatly manicured vineyards. The walk is steep, so enjoy the view as you go slowly. You'll stroll past an inviting porch swing and enter the living room–hospitality center where a tasting bar is arranged in a corner of the former dining room. The brief but informative tour departs from the tasting area, passes through the rooms on the first floor, and then moves on to the upper patio just beyond the front door. From there, you'll enjoy a splendid view across and down the valley no matter the season in which you're visiting.

The tour continues under the house in the barrel-lined stone cellar. The scent of fermenting grapes may hit you here more than in larger wineries because of the relatively small dimensions of this space. Because wine has been aged in the cellar since the 1880s, that aroma has permeated even the stone and timbers supporting the house.

Out into the daylight and up a gentle hill, you'll come to a newer stone building that houses the fermenting tanks. Most probably you will meet the winemaker, who is open to answering queries about techniques, cold stabilization, the harvest, or whatever is on your mind. The tour guides are extremely friendly, acting more like aunts welcoming visiting relatives than group leaders. The group numbers here tend to mirror the winery's small size—you will probably share the visit with six or fewer travelers. After visiting the fermentation area, a return to the tasting room completes the walking tour and a generous tasting ensues.

There is little wonder that St. Clement's charm has captured many TV commercial producers and that it is frequently mistaken for a bed and breakfast inn. It stands solitary on its hill, a reminder of the gracious way of life here more than a century ago.

ST. SUPÉRY VINEYARDS AND WINERY

St. Supéry Vineyards and Winery
8440 St. Helena Highway
Rutherford, CA 94573
(707) 963-4507 or (800) 942-0809
fax (707) 963-4526
Website: www.stsupery.com
Email: divinecab@stsupery.com

Winemaker: Michael Beaulac
Winery owners: Skalli family

Access
Location: On Highway 29 midway between the towns of Oakville and Rutherford, on the east side of the highway.

Hours open for visits and tastings: 10 A.M.–5:30 P.M. June through October, 10 A.M.–5 P.M. November through May, except major holidays.

Appointment necessary for tour? No. Tours at 11 A.M. and 1 and 3 P.M.

Wheelchairs accommodated? Yes.

Tastings
Charge for tasting with tour? $5. Charge for tasting without tour? $5 for four wines and lifetime tasting pass; $10 for three high-end wines (no tasting pass).

Typical wines offered: Napa Valley Sauvignon Blanc, Chardonnay, Merlot, Cabernet Sauvignon, and Moscato, plus Meritage wines and limited edition wines.

Sales of wine-related items? Yes.

Picnics and Programs
Picnic area open to the public? No.

Special events or wine-related programs? Art exhibits, garden tours, concerts, and wine classes.

Wedding gifts in the mid-nineteenth century were occasionally offered in the form of land, rather than lace tablecloths or family photos in silver frames. In fact, this fifty-six-acre winery in the midst of George C. Yount's original five-hundred-acre Rancho Caymus land grant was the dowry gift for Bartlett Vine's marriage to Ellen Yount. She was a daughter of George C. Yount, the prominent landowner who first planted grapestock in the Napa Valley. Later, in 1881, brothers Joseph and Louis Atkinson bought the land and built a home near the hundred-year-old oak tree that shaded a corner of the vineyard. When French winemaker Edward St. Supéry lived in the house, from 1904 to 1920, his home was a magnet for winemakers of the day—Charles Krug, Jacob Beringer, and Jacob Schram were frequent visitors.

A strong sense of history accompanies a visit to St. Supéry, despite the fact that the winery is one of the more recently established estates along Highway 29. Perhaps it is the juxtaposition of the new and the old: the state-of-the-art straight lines of the wine-production area contrast with the lush lawn and floral landscaping fronting the Queen Anne Victorian Atkinson house. Or perhaps it is the gracious, old-fashioned hospitality with which tourists are greeted. Among its several lures, the St. Supéry winery has appeal for all ages and wine-appreciation levels.

St. Supéry offers guided as well as unescorted tours. Especially if you arrive during harvest, don't miss the guided tour. It winds from the lobby of the modern winery out through the Atkinson house (which is open for tours only and is decorated with authentic 1880s furnishings appropriate for a summer home) and past a gazebo into the exhibition vineyard. There, visitors are encouraged to pick varieties of grapes grown for St. Supéry wines, fulfilling the unspoken but frequent dream of having a hand at "working the crush."

While in the vineyard, the tour guide discusses the Dollarhide Ranch, the winery's vineyard of fifteen hundred acres in Pope Valley, northeast of St. Helena. The size alone puts St. Supéry among the largest vineyards for land holdings.

From the vineyard, the tour returns to the production side of the operation. With a 536,000-gallon tank capacity and the ability to bottle 2,500 cases per day, it is no wonder that St. Supéry can produce 160,000 cases of its own wines as well as doing custom crush and bottling for other wineries—working to capacity, you could say.

As the tour continues on a wide catwalk over massive stainless-steel tanks, the well-trained guide points out icy buildup on some of the tank walls, due to cold stabilization of white and red wines. When the temperature is dropped well below normal, any sedi-

when they see a wooden model of a vineyard that is surrounded on four sides with descriptions of the operations of a vineyard year (see page 21).

"Smell-a-Vision" is a favorite learning device on the walk-around tour. Here, tourists can smell aromatic essences to help identify the same elements in wine. Using a special display, guests smell cedar, bell-pepper, cherry, and black-pepper scents related to red-wine aromas. White-wine "whiffs" are grapefruit, green olive, dried wildflower, and new-mown hay.

Moving from aromas to wine tasting is a natural step, one that is rewarded with samples of at least five wines. The well-appointed shop offers wines, including limited releases and large-format bottles, logo clothing, books on food, wine, and the Napa Valley, and other items related to wine and food.

Culture is very important to the directors of St. Supéry. Be sure to view the changing art shows on display in the entry and gallery. And, if you are in the valley for a few days, ask whether the winery is presenting any cultural events, such as a chamber music concert.

ment in the wine drops to the bottom of the tank and can be easily removed, eliminating visible tartrates. Another plus of a harvest tour here is the outdoor viewing platform directly above the hopper where grapes are received and sent to the crusher-stemmer.

Locals call the St. Supéry self-guided tour "touchy-feely," although the clearly defined walk in the air-conditioned, carpeted space is primarily geared to the senses of sight and smell.

All who previously thought that growing wine grapes was a simple pastime will quickly reconsider

SCHRAMSBERG VINEYARDS

Schramsberg Vineyards
1400 Schramsberg Road
Calistoga, CA 94515
(707) 942-4558 or (800) 877-3623
fax (707) 942-5943
Website: www.schramsberg.com
Email: info@schramsberg.com

Winemaker: Hugh Davies
Winery owner: The Davies Family

Access
Location: Five miles north of St. Helena
on Highway 29; turn west onto
Peterson and make a quick right onto
Schramsberg Road.

Hours open for visits and tastings:
Visitor's center open 10 A.M.–4 P.M.
daily, except New Year's Day and
Christmas.

Appointment necessary for tour? Yes.

Wheelchairs accommodated? Yes.

Tastings
Charge for tasting with tour? $20 for
four half-glasses, not deductible from
cost of purchased wine.
Charge for tasting without tour?
Tasting with tour only.

Typical wines offered: Blanc de Blancs,
Blanc de Noirs, Reserve, and J.
Schram.

Sales of wine-related items? Yes.
Clothing, bouchons, etched glasses,
and books.

Picnics and Programs
Picnic area open to the public? No.

Special events or wine-related
programs? Sparkling Wine
Symposium; Cellar Club.

The Schramsberg hillside winery and caves epitomize the romance of wine making in the Napa Valley. Very little has changed on the exterior of this estate since it was founded in 1862 by Jacob and Annie Schram, emigrés from Germany. But changes here have been made: in fact, Jamie Davies and her late husband, Jack, enhanced the property with Victorian gardens and expanded the underground tunnel system to two miles of storage for the sparkling wines made here.

Thousands of visitors travel here every year to encounter the source of Schramsberg's celebrated Napa Valley *méthode champenoise* (aged in the bottle) sparkling wines. The tourists come with the same interest in wine and lifestyle that beckoned Jack and Jamie Davies to the wine country when they left the Southern California corporate life.

"We call it Napa Valley Champagne," explains Jamie Davies, "because French Champagne is perceived as the finest of that country's sparkling wine. We didn't want to hint at lesser quality here."

Jamie lives in Jacob Schram's original Victorian home with a wide veranda overlooking cascading flowers and the entry to the caves. The home was built in the 1880s, coinciding with winery construction at Beringer, Chateau Montelena, Inglenook, and the estates now known as St. Clement and Spring Mountain.

From the 1860s through the turn of the last century, wineries flourished in the Napa Valley, with more than eighteen thousand acres planted to vines by 1900. It was during that early heyday of the local wine industry that Robert Louis Stevenson frequently visited Jacob Schram. Later he devoted a chapter to the Schramsberg estate in his *Silverado Squatters*. (For further information on the famous writer, visit the Robert Louis Stevenson Museum in the town of St. Helena.)

During Prohibition and with a variety of owners, the winery rested. Its hand-dug underground cellar system remained in disrepair until 1965, when the Davies couple came across the Schram Estate after an extensive search for a winery property. They purchased the neglected estate and set about planting Chardonnay, Pinot Noir, and Pinot Blanc vines.

The tour begins at the upper crush-pad area near the parking lot, below the private home. You will pass fragrant plantings of rosemary and other herbs, as well as mulberry trees and palm trees. Most Napa Valley palm trees were planted at the turn of the last century; they were considered exotic status symbols. As you drive the valley's length, note the placement of palms like tufted elephants' legs in the bright Napa sun. Many have been growing a century or longer.

Below the house, an amusing bronze statue of a rakish frog, Champagne flute in hand, seems to rise out of the lotus pond fronting the entrance to the caves. Once inside the visitors' center, you'll see numerous photos of VIPs in the worlds of politics, art, and music, all related to menus of dinners where

Schramsberg has been served since its first Blanc de Blancs release in 1969.

The cellars are well lit, with rows of poker-table green light fixtures illuminating the walls of Champagne bottles. At least two million bottles rest on their sides, with a hundred pounds of pressure in each bottle. The bottles remain dormant until the wine-maker decides the proper time for riddling, the turning action that moves the dead yeasts down to the neck of each bottle.

"We house up to six years of vintages of the reserves here," points out the tour guide, "and that's only one of our seven styles of Napa Valley sparkling wine."

Of all the caves in this valley, those at Schramsberg come closest to the ambiance of the catacombs of Paris and other such dank, romantic subterranean cellars. Moss clings to the walls and water oozes from the rocky mountainside.

If you're seeking a hands-on experience, do try the riddling exercise in the caves. Watching master riddler Ramon Viera give rows of Champagne bottles a one-sixth turn makes the symmetrical action seem effortless—until you try it. "Fingers only! Don't use your wrist!" cheerleads the tour guide as visitors volunteer to try their hand—rather, their fingers—at the art. And Ramon's twenty-seven years of riddling forty thousand to sixty thousand bottles daily suddenly make him a hero.

"What happens if a bottle drops?" asks a tourist. He learns that Champagne bottles are much heavier than standard wine bottles to counteract the fermenting pressure; however, a Champagne bottle would shatter into thousands of shards if dropped on cement.

During the tour, you'll learn that 30 percent of the pressure and 10 percent of the wine is lost with the disgorging action. After understanding the various stages of pressure a bottle must endure in the sparkling-wine process, one tourist remarked that she would never again complain about the cost of a bottle of Napa Valley sparkling wine. The tour guide will explain that as the bottles' metal caps are removed, the frozen plug of sediment flies out of the bottle. Then a small *dosage* of sugar and brandy or cognac or wine is added to sweeten the sparkling wine, followed by immediate corking and labeling.

To depart the two and one-half underground cave miles and head for the tasting room, you'll retrace some steps through the caves. Some say that exiting the cave feels like departing the Tunnel of Love.

SILVERADO VINEYARDS

Silverado Vineyards
6121 Silverado Trail
Napa, CA 94558
(707) 257-1770
fax (707) 257-1538
Website: www.silveradovineyards.com
Email: info@silveradovineyards.com

Winemaker: Jon Emmerich
Winemaster/General Manager:
Jack Stuart
Winery owners: Ron and Diane
Disney Miller

Access
Location: One mile south of Yountville
Crossroad. The winery is on the west
side of the Silverado Trail, clearly
marked.

Hours open for visits and tastings:
10:30 A.M.–5 P.M. daily, except
New Year's Day, Thanksgiving,
and Christmas.

Appointment necessary for tour? Yes;
24-hour notice preferred. Tours at
10:30 A.M. and 2:30 P.M. daily.

Wheelchairs accommodated? Yes.

Tastings
Charge for tasting with tour? Charge
for tour is $10 and includes tasting.
Charge for tasting without tour? $7
to $15 per tasting.

Typical wines offered: Sauvignon
Blanc, Chardonnay, Rosato, San
Giovese, Zinfandel, Merlot, and
Cabernet Sauvignon.

Sales of wine-related items? Yes.

Picnics and Programs
Picnic area open to the public? No.

Special events or wine-related
programs? Silverado Vineyards' Wine
Club. In-house events available for
corporate groups only.

Take a wide turn onto a gentle ascent west of the Silverado Trail and follow the road's curve to the hilltop. There you will find one of the more gracious wineries in the Napa Valley. Once you've settled inside the welcoming tasting room, timbered with 150-year-old Douglas fir beams and terraced with terra-cotta pavers, you might draw the conclusion that the owners of this vineyard spared no expense to create the architecture, the vineyards, and the wine—and you would be correct. Diane Disney Miller and her husband, Ron Miller, purchased two neighboring vineyards in Napa's Stags Leap District during the late 1970s with the goal of "creating something beautiful from this land."

Silverado was constructed in 1981 when Diane's mother, Lillian Disney, the widow of Walt Disney, was alive. In the entire winery visit, there is only one understated reference to the imaginative animated world of the man whose dreams helped to make this wine-country center possible. Before entering the massive "employee dining room," also known as the board room and/or the main dining room, look to your right to see an Andy Warhol rendition of Mickey Mouse. Within the expansive room, look for the stained glass window on the western wall. In fact, the whole winery is graced with original contemporary or early California art, reflecting the interests of its owners.

During the tour, you'll learn that the winery has continued to grow considerably since its early days in the 1980s. The fruit for various Silverado vintages, including Sauvignon Blanc, Chardonnay, Merlot, Sangiovese, and Cabernet Sauvignon, now comes from over three hundred vineyard acres, with grapes from Stags Leap, Atlas Peak, Carneros, and Mt. George, south of Napa. In all cases, Silverado's winemaster/general manager, Jack Stuart, insists that the wines' character and quality are rooted in the vineyards. Jon Emmerich, the winemaker here, has followed a classic path to achieve his role today. After graduating from the University of California, Davis, in 1987 with a B.S. in fermentation science, Emmerich worked a harvest at Stag's Leap Wine Cellars. He then

spent a year each at Conn Creek Winery and Sebastiani before moving to Silverado Vineyards in 1990, where he worked with Stuart for ten years of training before moving into the winemaker position. Much like the professional chefs hopscotching from kitchen to kitchen in Napa Valley's famed restaurants, it is necessary to work in a variety of wineries to have the background to be a respected winemaker today.

All the Silverado Vineyards wines are estate-grown and hand-harvested. When it comes to wine, the term *estate* refers to land that produces wine from its own grapes, and the use of the term is highly protected by law. In this time when wines are often blends of grape juices from vineyards held by a variety of owners, the Napa Valley is one source of many estate-bottled wines. Silverado bottles only wines from its own grapes, making its wines 100 percent estate vintages.

The friendly tour guide will lead you through the public rooms upstairs. He will point out a quote from *The Silverado Squatters*, by the Silverado Trail's turn-of-the-last-century author/resident Robert Louis

Stevenson: "The beginning of vine planting is like the beginning of mining for the precious metals: The wine-grower also 'prospects.'" You'll be led down to the cellars where French oak barrels are stacked five high, two rows wide. As each winemaker requests certain toastiness within the barrels for a wine, the guide will discuss the medium toast for these barrels. You may feel a slight misting (welcome on some of our particularly hot summer days); know that the gentle spray is there to increase the humidity in the room when the temperature is rising. The more humidity, the higher the chances of keeping wine in the barrels from evaporating.

If the sleek Italian bottling mechanism is up and running, you'll see some real action! Eighty-one bottles a minute, three thousand cases a day, zip through the steel bottling path as the bottles are rinsed, filled, labeled, corked, foiled, and boxed.

Back in the tasting room, you'll sip various vintages while you enjoy the spectacular view of the valley, no matter what the season. You'll be looking down at Yountville Crossroad and all the vineyards surrounding that area, particularly the estate vineyards, source of some of the very wine you'll be enjoying.

STAG'S LEAP WINE CELLARS

Stag's Leap Wine Cellars
5766 Silverado Trail
Napa, CA 94558
(707) 944-2020
fax (707) 257-7501
Website: www.stagsleapwinecellars.com
Email: retail@cask23.com

Winemaker: Warren Winiarski
Winery owners: Warren and Barbara
Winiarski

Access
Location: From the town of Napa,
take Trancas Street to the Silverado
Trail; the winery is 7 miles north on
the east side.

Hours open for visits and tastings:
10 A.M.–4:30 P.M. daily, except New
Year's Day, Easter, Thanksgiving,
and Christmas.

Appointment necessary for tour? Yes.

Wheelchairs accommodated? Yes.

Tastings
Charge for tasting with tour? $10 for
Portfolio Tasting of four wines; $30 for
estate wines, including a logo glass to
keep. Offered at 10:30 A.M. and 2 P.M.;
no charge for tours.
Charge for tasting without tour?
As above.

Typical wines offered: Current releases
of Sauvignon Blanc, White Riesling,
Chardonnay, Cabernet Sauvignon,
Merlot, and Petite Syrah.

Sales of wine-related items? Yes.

Picnics and Programs
Picnic area open to the public? No.

Special events or wine-related
programs? The *Stag's Leap Wine
Cellars News* notifies those on the
mailing list of winery activities and
special events.

There is a sense of serious dedication to integrity and fine wine making imparted during a visit to Warren and Barbara Winiarski's Stag's Leap Wine Cellars. Since 1970, Warren Winiarski, a former University of Chicago political science lecturer, has insisted on stressing his vines and tightening the space between rows of Cabernet Sauvignon vines, so the roots will stretch as deep as thirty feet in soil he rarely irrigates. This soil lies on the south end of the Stags Leap District, which runs along the Silverado Trail from Clos du Val (just south of Stag's Leap Wine Cellars) to the Oakville Cross Road. To the workers at the winery as well as the Winiarskis, that soil and the grapes harvested annually from the vines are the source of happiness and success.

It was Stag's Leap Wine Cellars' 1973 Cabernet Sauvignon that took highest honors during the pivotal Paris blind tasting in June 1976, when a Napa Valley Chardonnay (Chateau Montelena) and this Cabernet changed the global sea of opinion and earned waves of adulation for California wine. The truly amazing fact is that the Winiarskis' grapes had been plucked from three-year-old vines, usually considered too immature to produce complex flavor. "That winning put us on the map and showed that Napa Valley is a place that makes fine wines," mentions tour guide Adrian Rincon.

As you would expect, a man who takes his wines so seriously mirrors his philosophy in tours at this winery. The basic tour here runs about a half-hour; however, Stag's Leap Wine Cellars draws true wine connoisseurs as visitors, and their questions often demand detailed explanation. Count on an hour if you are scheduling the day.

You will walk under ancient oak trees based with profuse plantings of ornamental strawberries and wild roses. In summer, the bouquet from the flowers can be overpowering. You will move past the roof-covered fermentation tanks and on to the original crush pad. Occasionally Barbara Winiarski will greet guests and answer a few questions.

"You know, we never imagined we'd need a second phone, much less a second building," she commented about the physical growth of the winery since its 1972 opening. "That's why the five structures on the property have such basic names: Building 1, Building 2, and so on." There is little room here donated to frivolous extras, but tourists will experience an active small winery with a mom-and-pop feel.

Tour guides are extremely well informed and cover such topics as irrigation systems, acidity, Brix levels (the level of natural sugar within the grapes), the effects of drought, and the mix of clay, volcanic soil, and pebbles that creates ideal soil conditions for grow-

ing Cabernet Sauvignon grapes. You will pass through the indoor-outdoor fermentation area and then walk uphill to the French oak barrel-aging building.

Workers in knee-high rubber boots continue their winery work, moving hoses, climbing the pyramids of barrels to "top off" any air space, and hosing the cement floors to maintain the impeccable conditions necessary to wine.

Discussion will continue about grape types, malolactic fermentation, growers, and microclimates. For some tourists, this visit will include more than they want to know; for others, this will be winery-tour heaven.

The tour concludes at the long wooden table in Building 2 where various vintages are poured. If you wish to taste Hawk Crest, the winery's companion label, just request it at the tasting table. The tasting moves in a standard pattern: first the white wines, followed by the heavier, more tannic red wines. Mineral water is available for designated drivers. By the time of tasting, the small, disparate group of visitors has had a chance to meet and there is a sense of camaraderie, with an occasional exchange of addresses.

The shady seating area on the face of the winery property just above the parking area offers tables and chairs in a garden setting. This can be a quiet rest stop for motorists and bicyclists as well.

Note: There is some confusion concerning punctuation in the names Stag's Leap Wine Cellars and Stags' Leap Winery and the appellation Stags Leap District. To clarify: the Stags Leap District appellation was designated officially in the late 1980s and is spelled without an apostrophe. Beringer's Stags' Leap Winery connotes a number of stags, whereas the Winiarskis' name refers to a single stag.

Sterling Vineyards
1111 Dunaweal Lane
Calistoga, CA 94515
(707) 942-3344 or (800) 726-6136
fax (888) 321-5028
Website: www.sterlingvineyards.com
Email: See website

Winemaker: Robert Hunter
Winery owner: Diageo Chateau &
Estate Wines

Access
Location: One mile south of Calistoga
off Dunaweal Lane, between Highway
29 and the Silverado Trail.

Hours open for visits and tastings:
10:30 A.M.–4:30 P.M. daily, except New
Year's Day, Easter, and Thanksgiving.

Appointment necessary for tour? No.

Wheelchairs accommodated? Yes.

Tastings
Charge for tasting with tour? $10,
including sky-tram ride to winery,
self-paced tour, and sit-down tasting
of four wines.
Charge for tasting without tour?
As above.

Typical wines offered: Current releases
of Chardonnay, Sauvignon Blanc,
Merlot, and Cabernet Sauvignon.

Sales of wine-related items? Yes.

Picnics and Programs
Picnic area open to the public? No.

Special events or wine-related
programs? Special events for members
of Sterling Vineyards Cellar Club: sum-
mer picnic, Christmas party, and more.

STERLING VINEYARDS

The panoramic vista from the bell-tower deck at Sterling Vineyards is one of the most spectacular in the Napa Valley. From there you will see mountain ranges encircling the valley floor, with a sweep broad enough to include Highway 29 and the Silverado Trail in one glance. During the spring, rust-colored farmsteads and bright-blue reservoirs contrast with a central carpet of yellow mustard flowers blooming at the base of dormant rootstock. And in the Mediterranean style of this winery, olive trees and cypresses frame the extensive property.

When the winery was built, in 1971, the idea was to create a place of prominence by placing its pure white arches, towers, and castlelike walls high above the valley floor. At the same time, architect Martin Waterfield constructed a cool mountainside area for the chai (barrel-aging area) by building it vertically into the hill and lighting it through gemlike stained glass windows.

Because of the labyrinthine driving paths and the narrow roads to the top of the estate, a sky tram (ten dollars per person) was devised to transport visitors over gardens, vineyards, and a small lake to the arrival dock, where a self-guided tour begins. Follow the informational placards to learn about wine making in the grand style. Sterling, which is owned by Diageo Chateau & Estate Wines, is now the largest grape grower in the Napa Valley. It produces eleven varietal wines here from grapes grown on its 2,500 acres of Napa Valley vines, and it has a fermentation

capacity of almost 500,000 gallons. The signs will direct you from station to station and, even on a busy day, you'll rarely have the sense of being in a crowd.

There is quite a bit of walking up and down stairs on this visit, including a steep climb to the final tasting-room stop. On a blisteringly hot day, take it slowly.

Once in the tasting-room area, you can relax in the spacious air-conditioned interior. From the terraces outside, you'll be able to see through pines, redwoods, and some oaks up-valley toward Calistoga. Clos Pegase winery is in view, as is the imposing Mount St. Helena, the tallest peak in the San Francisco Bay Area.

While in the visitors' center, you'll also see St. Dunstan's dining room off one windowed side of the white winery structure, available for private dinners.

By the time of descent via tram to the parking lot, you will have learned a considerable amount about wine making and you'll have been to the top of the world in the middle of the valley.

SUTTER HOME WINERY

Sutter Home Winery
277 St. Helena Highway
St. Helena, CA 94574
(707) 963-3104, ext. 4208
fax (707) 967-9184
Websites: www.sutterhome.com
or www.tfewines.com
Email: info@sutterhome.com

Winemakers: Sutter Home Wines—
Jim Huntsinger; Trinchero Family
Estates—Joe Shirley
Winery owners: Trinchero family

Access

Location: One mile south of St. Helena
on the west side of Highway 29, at the
large white Victorian.

Hours open for visits and tastings:
10 A.M.–5 P.M. daily, except New Year's
Day, Easter, and Christmas.

Appointment necessary for tour? No.
Self-guided garden tours during open
hours.

Wheelchairs accommodated? In tasting
room, not in gardens.

Tastings

Charge for tasting with tour? Three
choices of tastings: complimentary
tasting; "proprietor series"—$5 with
a keepsake glass, $7 for reserve wines
with a keepsake glass.
Charge for tasting without tour?
As above.

Typical wines offered: White Zinfandel,
Chardonnay, Sauvignon Blanc, White
Merlot, Merlot, and Cabernet
Sauvignon.

Sales of wine-related items? Yes.

Picnics and Programs

Picnic area open to the public? No.

Special events or wine-related
programs? Wine club.

If an easy self-tour is your goal in visiting a winery, Sutter Home is an ideal destination. The visit to this winery, known largely for its White Zinfandel but home to a wide range of wines, consists of walking around the perimeter of a large room with a central wine-tasting bar. During the tasting, you have the option to discuss and taste Sutter Home and Trinchero Family Estates wines with knowledgeable winery staff members. Call ahead for this option.

Inside the winery's visitors' center, there is no treatment of vineyards and grapes, with the exception of a display of old wine-production machines, some photos of wine-making procedures, and a placard that presents the story of the winery. Wine is described as an enhancement to daily life in the style of the good old days.

But the natural is also celebrated, in the present-day garden just outside the visitors' center, which is alive with eight hundred varieties of flowers, trees, and plants in the beds surrounding the 1884 Victorian home on the property. Garden tours are available and well worth the walk. You'll see beds of exquisite roses, scented geraniums, free-form wisteria, butterfly bushes, and trees such as weeping flowering cherry and Japanese maple. If photographing flowers is a hobby for you, be sure to visit Sutter Home midsummer for the best color and floral varieties.

Although the home is closed to the public, tourists are encouraged to rest in the garden gazebo and relax, remembering a time when life was slower.

The Trinchero family, which now owns Sutter Home as well as Trinchero Family Estates, traces the winery's history back to 1890, when it was the first wooden winery in the valley. "The story of Sutter Home is a slice of Americana," reads the notice at the interior entry to the tasting room. "Its fate rose and fell with impacts of World Wars I and II, with Prohibition, the Depression, the Great Immigration of Europeans to the United States and the San Francisco earthquake and fire of 1906. That year, Sutter Home, every acre, every building, was sold for $10 gold." Today's Sutter Home, which rose to success on the wings of White Zinfandel's popularity in the 1970s and 1980s, is one of the most profitable wineries in the country. Its actual (and huge) wine-production area is a few miles away, off Zinfandel Lane, where nearly ten million cases of wine are produced annually from Napa Valley and other California grapes. But the winery center on Highway 29 just south of St. Helena continues to draw thousands of tourists who yearn to trace the roots of their favorite wine—"White Zin."

TREFETHEN VINEYARDS

Trefethen Vineyards
1160 Oak Knoll Avenue
Napa, CA 94558
(707) 255-7700
fax (707) 255-0793
Website: www.trefethen.com
Email: winery@trefethen.com

Winemaker: Peter Luthi
Winery owners: Janet and John
Trefethen

Access
Location: On Highway 29, 2 miles
north of the city of Napa, turn right
on Oak Knoll Avenue. Trefethen is the
first entrance on the left.

Hours open for visits and tastings:
10 A.M.–4:30 P.M. daily, except Easter,
Thanksgiving, and Christmas.

Appointment necessary for tour? Yes.

Wheelchairs accommodated? Yes.

Tastings
Charge for tasting with tour? Some
complimentary tastings. Fee for
Reserve and limited-release tastings.
Charge for tasting without tour? Yes;
call for prices.

Typical wines offered: Dry Riesling,
Chardonnay, Merlot, Cabernet
Sauvignon, Library Selections, and
Reserve wines.

Sales of wine-related items? Yes,
including books, logo glasses, and
apparel.

Picnics and Programs
Picnic area open to the public? No.

Special events or wine-related
programs? Trefethen Connection
Wine Club.

The Trefethen family has a deep pride in its six hundred contiguous acres of vineyards, one of the largest plots under single ownership within the Napa Valley. As a result, tourists quickly learn the history of the land and how it relates to the winery estate.

The drive onto the property from Oak Knoll Avenue can be reached easily from the Silverado Trail or Highway 29. As you enter, signs clearly mark the various grape varieties—Pinot Noir, Chardonnay, Cabernet Sauvignon. The old winery dominates the property with its massive form, painted the Tuscan orange of a winter sunset.

Founded in 1886, the former Eshcol winery was the earliest three-story gravity-flow winery in the county. It produced wine until 1940, with a hiatus during Prohibition (1919–1933), during which time the government granted permission for making sacramental or personal-use wines only.

Vestiges of earlier days are evident in the visitors' entry room, where the tour begins. You'll see photos of the land when it was planted to walnut and prune orchards, as it was in 1968, when Gene and Katie Trefethen chose this six hundred-acre parcel of land with the dream of remodeling the Eshcol winery and planting grapes once again. "We are a destination winery," declares a guide to a small group of tourists. "Fifty percent of our visitors already know Trefethen wines and are willing to drive here to find us," he adds, "and we prefer people who are interested in wine." There is the advantage in an intimate-size group that you can stop at any point and ask questions, which are encouraged and are answered in depth.

This is a "backward" tour, in the sense that the first areas you'll visit—the barrel-aging rooms—are not first in the sequence of wine making. But since Trefethen originally was a gravity-flow winery, it makes sense to see barrels where they used to rest over a hundred years ago.

In a gravity-flow winery, grapes are crushed, stemmed, and fermented on the top floor. The fermented juice is next aged in barrels on the second floor, then rolled to the ground level for bottling and shipping.

The stairs to the second floor of the winery are narrow. You'll view a majority of small oak barrels, which hold enough wine to fill 325,000 750-milliliter bottles. Note the silicone bungs in the barrels. These barrel stoppers are made of an inert material that provides a tighter seal than the standard wooden bungs.

Whenever you tour Napa Valley wineries, you will hear discussion of the "toast" of the oak in various wines. Trefethen Vineyards makes the effort to discriminate among the various stages of toastiness: there is a display of woods from six different oak barrel interiors, each of which has been carefully charred to develop a certain level of toasted oak flavor. Later, during wine tasting, the tour guide will point out the "toast" quality of the various wines.

Moving from the main building, the tour passes the crush pad and crusher-stemmer. During harvest, you are in clear view of grape delivery and all the swift stages that take place from arrival of the hand-picked grapes in open-topped gondolas (fruit-bearing trailers) to fermentation. The fermentation tanks, bottling line, and other stages of production are quite accessible. "Everything you see," points out the guide, "from vine to bottle, is done on our land. Therefore, it can be called 'estate bottled'—all our wines are estate bottled."

V. SATTUI WINERY

V. Sattui Winery
1111 White Lane
St. Helena, CA 94574
(707) 963-7774 or (800) 799-2337
fax (707) 963-4324
Website: www.vsattui.com
Email: info@vsattui.com

Winemaker: Rick Rosenbrand
Winery owner: Daryl Sattui

Access

Location: On Highway 29 at White Lane, a half-mile south of St. Helena.

Hours open for visits and tastings: 9 A.M.–6 P.M. daily, March through October; 9 A.M.–5 P.M. daily, November through February, except Christmas Day.

Appointment necessary for tour? Not for self-guided tours; private tours and groups do require appointments for tour and tasting: $80 minimum, $8 per person.

Wheelchairs accommodated? Yes.

Tastings

Charge for tasting with tour? $8. Charge for tasting without tour? As above.

Typical wines offered: Sauvignon Blanc, Chardonnay, Johannesburg Riesling, Gamay Rouge, Zinfandel, Cabernet Sauvignon, and California Madeira.

Sales of wine-related items? Yes.

Picnics and Programs

Picnic area open to the public? Yes. Picnicking for deli (on premises) customers only.

Special events or wine-related programs? The Wine of the Month program; Cellar Club private tasting for members.

Cheese and picnics, picnics and cheese. Napa Valley tourists' first impressions of the V. Sattui Winery, just south of St. Helena, relate to picnics, due to the two acres of shaded tables and benches fronting Highway 29. Beds of flowers, ancient oak trees, and a wine-tasting room and delicatessen enhance the visual invitation to turn off the road and relax.

Since the Napa Valley weather is relatively clement, about three hundred thousand visitors take advantage of the picnic area year-round. An Italian-style stone building dominates the land, with multilevel terraces, porches, and fountains decorating the front of the building.

This winery (built in 1975, although it appears older) is a far cry from Vittorio Sattui's Bryant Avenue Winery in San Francisco's North Beach. That company produced wine from 1885 to 1921 and then closed due to Prohibition. It was not until Vittorio's great-grandson Daryl Sattui reestablished the winery and moved it to St. Helena that the family name was again affiliated with wine.

The tour at V. Sattui is an extremely relaxed self-tour. As you walk the property and visit the various levels of the winery, you'll find signs describing the history of the ancient artifacts arranged outdoors, such as antique carts that used to transport wine in barrels. You are free to roam, to picnic, and to shop in the large retail store that offers breads, cheeses, wine, deli-style foods, and wine-related items. In fact, V. Sattui is one of the largest distributors of imported cheese in Northern California.

Despite the picnic atmosphere, the emphasis here is on making wine of fine quality. There is a barrel-lined underground stone wine cellar where weddings, private tastings, and meetings take place. The winery produces thirty thousand cases annually and keeps its overhead low by selling all its wine through the tasting room, along with cheese and picnics, picnics and cheese.

RESOURCES

RESOURCES

Note: All resources are in the 707 telephone area code.

CHAMBERS OF COMMERCE

CALISTOGA CHAMBER
OF COMMERCE
1458 Lincoln Avenue #9, Calistoga
942-6333
office@calistogachamber.com
www.calistogafun.com

NAPA CHAMBER OF COMMERCE
1556 First Street, Napa
226-7455
info@napachamber.org
www.napachamber.org

ST. HELENA CHAMBER
OF COMMERCE
1010 Main Street, Suite A, St. Helena
963-4456
www.sthelena.com

YOUNTVILLE CHAMBER
OF COMMERCE
6516 Yount Street, Yountville
944-0904
yountvl@aol.com
www.yountville.com

EDUCATIONAL SOURCES

CAKEBREAD CELLARS
8300 St. Helena Highway, Rutherford
963-5221 or (800) 588-0298
www.cakebread.com

CULINARY CONVERGENCE
Far Niente Winery
1350 Acacia Drive, Oakville
944-2861
www.farniente.com

THE CULINARY INSTITUTE
OF AMERICA AT GREYSTONE
2555 Main Street, St. Helena
(800) 333-9242
www.ciachef.edu

MASTER SERIES ON FOOD
AND WINE
Beringer Vineyards
2000 Main Street, St. Helena
963-7115
www.beringer.com

MEADOWOOD WINE CENTER
Meadowood
900 Meadowood Lane, St. Helena
963-3646
www.meadowood.com
(Groups of six to eight)

NAPA VALLEY COOKING SCHOOL
Napa Valley College,
Upper Valley Campus
1088 College Avenue, St. Helena
967-2930
www.napacommunityed.org/
cookingschool

PACIFIC UNION COLLEGE
1 Angwin Ave, Angwin
965-6311

ROBERT MONDAVI GREAT
CHEFS PROGRAM
Robert Mondavi Winery
7801 St. Helena Highway, Oakville
251-4097
www.robertmondavi.com

LIBRARIES

CALISTOGA LIBRARY
1108 Myrtle Street, Calistoga
942-4833
www.co.napa.ca.us/library/
calistoga_library.htm

NAPA COUNTY LIBRARY
580 Coombs Street, Napa
253-4243
www.co.napa.ca.us/library/
napa_main_library.htm

NAPA VALLEY WINE LIBRARY
1492 Library Lane, St. Helena
(within St. Helena Library)
963-5145
www.napawinelibrary.org

ST. HELENA LIBRARY
1492 Library Lane, St. Helena
963-5244
www.shpl.org

YOUNTVILLE LIBRARY
6548 Yount Street, Yountville
944-1888
www.co.napa.ca.us/library/yountville_
library.htm

MUSEUMS

BALE GRIST MILL
California State Park System
Three miles north of St. Helena (3369
N Street) on Highway 29, on the west
side of the road
942-4575
www.parks.ca.gov

CAROLYN PARR NATURE CENTER
3107 Browns Valley Road, Napa
255-6465

COPIA: THE AMERICAN CENTER
FOR WINE, FOOD, AND THE ARTS
500 First Street, Napa
(888) 51-COPIA
info@copia.org
www.copia.org

THE DIROSA PRESERVE:
ART AND NATURE
5200 Carneros Highway, Napa
226-5991
dirosa@napanet.net
www.dirosapreserve.org

THE HESS COLLECTION
4411 Redwood Road, Napa
255-1144
info@hesscollection.com
www.hesscollection.com

NAPA FIREFIGHTERS MUSEUM
1201 Main Street, Napa
259-0609

NAPA VALLEY MUSEUM
55 Presidents Circle, Yountville
944-0500
www.napavalleymuseum.org

OFF THE PRESERVE
1142 Main St., Napa
253-8300

ROBERT LOUIS STEVENSON
MUSEUM
At the Silverado Museum
1490 Library Lane, St. Helena
963-3757

SHARPSTEEN MUSEUM
1311 Washington Street, Calistoga
942-5911
admin@sharpsteen-museum.org
www.sharpsteen-museum.org

NEWSPAPERS

THE CALISTOGA TRIBUNE
1360 Lincoln Avenue, Calistoga 94515
942-5181
calistogatribune@aol.com

NAPA VALLEY REGISTER
1615 Second Street, Napa
226-3711
napanews@napanews.com
www.napanews.com

ST. HELENA STAR
1328 Main Street, St. Helena
963 2731
www.sthelenastar.com

THE WEEKLY CALISTOGAN
Po Box 346, St. Helena
942-6242
www.weeklycalistogan.com

MAGAZINES

THE VINE NAPA VALLEY
570 Gateway Drive, Napa 94558
224-5033
www.napavalleymagazine.com

TOURING
AND
WINE MAKING

TOURING AND WINE MAKING

ON TOURING WINERIES

Touring most Napa Valley wineries includes a nominal charge for the wines tasted. Occasionally, the charge includes a wine glass bearing a winery's logo. Some wineries offer gratis tastings.

Like restaurants, many wineries prefer to know their guest count, for obvious reasons. Although phone numbers are rarely taken when you book a tour, it is polite to call in to cancel. A tour guide may be brought in just for your party, particularly at the smaller wineries.

It is ideal to arrive at least five minutes before a tour. This leaves adequate time to locate and join the tour group, which may be out in the vineyard or in the barrel room.

In most cases, it is acceptable to arrive just before a tour and join in, but at wineries that request reservations, politeness suggests calling ahead, even that same morning.

Stay with the group, remembering that these are working wineries.

Expect noise from tractors, bottling machines, forklifts, and other equipment. In other words, be prepared for action.

On attire: casual clothing is the norm. After all, you'll be visiting working areas that often include newly turned earth or moist floors. Even on a blisteringly hot day, you may wish to bring a light wrap for touring the caves and wineries. They are air-conditioned to around fifty-five degrees, whether by nature or by machines, and the contrast in temperature is noticeable.

On footwear: it's a good idea to wear rubber-soled shoes. Since the winery business must be as sanitary as the dairy business, cleanliness is extremely important. Therefore, the floors of the winery are frequently wet from hosings. Also, closed-toe shoes are recommended for winery tours that include walking in the vineyard.

Some people collect etched wine glasses from the various wineries that sell such stemware.

If you wish to know how to find a certain wine in your hometown, do not hesitate to ask the tour guide. Small wineries are willing to talk to distributors in specific areas; large wineries don't need to.

It's not necessary to drink all the wine offered during a tasting. Use the dump buckets or spit buckets that are placed on the tasting bars for that purpose.

During any tour, expect a variety of levels of wine knowledgeability among the visitors. Don't be shy about asking questions.

Tour guides are often excellent sources for restaurant recommendations.

It is illegal to serve wine to minors, which includes anyone under the age of twenty-one.

There is no smoking in cellars or tasting rooms.

In most cases, you are encouraged to take photographs.

ON WINE AND WINE MAKING

Wine is fermented grape juice.

There is only one harvest annually, in the autumn in the Northern Hemisphere.

The local name for the harvest is "the crush."

The vintage year on a bottle refers to the year the grapes were picked.

Wine derives its natural sugar from the fruit itself; it is illegal to add sugar to still wines in California.

Grapes do not like "wet feet." There is little irrigation in the miles of vineyards. The grape rootstock has long roots, which seek the natural water level as deep as thirty feet underground.

Every state in the nation, except Alaska, grows grapes to make wine.

California grows more than 75 percent of the country's wine grapes, 90 percent of its table grapes, and all its raisin grapes.

Napa County encompasses 485,120 acres in total, and just 45,275 acres are planted in vineyards, which yield only 4 percent of the state's wine grapes.

To store wine while driving in the valley, keep it upright within the car (presuming you have not opened the bottle). The temperature inside a closed automobile can easily reach 110 degrees. Do not store wine in the trunk, particularly during extreme heat; the trunk will act as an oven and actually cook the wine.

A telltale sign that the wine has been overheated is a leaking bottle. This is caused by the contraction and expansion of the cork in response to the drastic change in temperature.

One plastic lug holds forty pounds of fruit.

Sparkling wine is popularly served in stemware called a flute. The flat coupe-shaped Champagne glasses popular in the past were said to have been based on the form of Marie Antoinette's left breast.

Notice the shapes of still wine bottles. Those with "sloping shoulders" are based on techniques used originally in the Burgundy region of France. Those with "square shoulders" are based on wines of the Bordeaux region. Historically, the reason for shouldering wine bottles was for tax purposes: the tax collector could define the source of the wine by "reading the shoulders."

Wine is the only alcoholic beverage that improves with aging after bottling and corking. September 1 is often the release date for new wines and their prices.

Check with your tour guide about shipping wine home. In most cases, it is illegal to ship from the winery, and there are limits on mailing wine to certain states at this time. There are local wine shops and shipping companies that can handle the transport process for you if you live in a state that allows shipping.

These are the graduated sizes of wine bottles:

Half-bottle (Tenth)	.375 milliliters
Standard bottle	.750 milliliters
Magnum	.2 standard bottles
	1.5 liters
Double magnum	.4 standard bottles
	3 liters
Jeroboam	.6 standard bottles
	4.5 liters
Rehoboam	.6 bottles Champagne
	4.5 liters
Methuselah	.8 bottles Champagne
	6 liters
Imperial	.8 standard bottles
	6 liters
Salmanazar	.12 standard bottles
	9 liters
Balthazar	.16 standard bottles
	12 liters
Nebuchadnezzar	.20 standard bottles
	15 liters

ON BARRELS

Wine-aging barrels, cut in half, are often available for use as, for example, planters or table bases. Ask your tour guide whether the winery has any for sale or where they can be found nearby.

A "barrel tasting" refers to tasting wine directly out of the aging barrel before the wine is bottled. (It has nothing to do with tasting the barrel itself!)

A full barrel contains 498 pounds of wine. Including the 50-pound barrel, the weight is near 550 pounds.

New French barrels cost around $700.

New American barrels cost around $350.

One French barrel holds sixty gallons, the equivalent of twenty-five cases of wine.

Each case of wine holds nine liters of beverage.

American oak barrels are made in Tennessee, Kentucky, Ohio, and California.

French barrels have full, broad "bellies" with wide space between steel bands at the center; American barrels are more uniformly shaped, with steel bands at relatively even widths across the barrel.

Barrels are often stacked on wooden triangular wedges. You also will see them on wooden pallets, steel squared-off frames, and wooden frames.

If red-wine barrels seem old and stained compared to pristine white-wine barrels, your observation is correct. Grape juice for red wines is colored by steeping it in the grape skins. The resultant red color stains barrels and gives them an appearance of age.

DIRECTORY

A DIRECTORY OF
NAPA VALLEY WINERIES

Note: All wineries are in the 707 telephone area code

ACACIA WINERY
2750 Las Amigas Road
Napa 94559
226-9991
info@acaciawinery.com
www.acaciawinery.com

AETNA SPRINGS CELLARS
7227 Pope Valley Road
Pope Valley 94574
965-2675
kimsey@aetnaspringscellars.com
www.aetnaspringscellars.com

ALTAMURA WINERY
1700 Wooden Valley Road
Napa 94558
253-2000

AMICI CELLARS
15 Christine Court
St. Helena 94574
967-9560
jeff@amicicellars.com
www.amicicellars.com

AMIZETTA VINEYARDS
1099 Greenfield Road
St. Helena 94574
963-1460
sclark@amizetta.com
www.amizetta.com

ANDERSON'S CONN VALLEY VINEYARDS
680 Rossi Road
St. Helena 94574
963-8600
cvvinfo@connvalleyvineyards.com
www.connvalleyvineyards.com

S. ANDERSON VINEYARDS
1473 Yountville Cross Road
Yountville 94599
944-8642
info@sandersonvineyards.com
www.4bubbly.com

ANDRETTI WINERY
4162 Big Ranch Road
Napa 94558
259-6777 or 261-1717
www.andrettiwinery.com

ARDENTE WINERY
2929 Atlas Peak Road
Napa 94558
226-7669
info@ardentewinery.com
www.ardentewinery.com

ARNS WINERY
601 Mund Road
St. Helena 94574
963-3429
arnswine@napanet.net

ARROYO WINERY
2361 Greenwood Avenue
Calistoga 94515
942-6995
info@vincentarroyowinery.com
http://vincentarroyowinery.com

ARTESA WINERY
1345 Henry Road
Napa 94559
224-1668
info@artesawinery.com
www.artesawinery.com

DAVID ARTHUR VINEYARDS
1521 Sage Canyon Road
St. Helena 94574
963-5190
davwine@aol.com
www.davidarthur.com

ATALON WINERY
7600 St. Helena Highway
Oakville 94562
800-224-4090
atalon.info@atalon.com
www.atalon.com

ATLAS PEAK VINEYARDS
3700 Soda Canyon Road
Napa 94558
252-7971
apv_info@atlaspeak.com
www.atlaspeak.com

AZALEA SPRINGS WINERY
P.O. Box 1089
Calistoga 94515
942-4811
www.azaleasprings.com

BACIO DIVINO
P.O. Box 131
Rutherford 94573
942-8101
cloudy@baciodivino.com
www.baciodivino.com

BALLENTINE VINEYARDS
2820 St. Helena Highway North
St. Helena 94574
963-7919
info@ballentinevineyards.com
www.ballentinevineyards.com

BARNETT VINEYARDS
4070 Spring Mountain Road
St. Helena 94574
963-7075
winecellar@barnettvineyards.com
www.barnettvineyards.com

BAYVIEW CELLARS
1150 Bayview Avenue
Napa 94558
255-8544
www.bayviewine.com

BEAUCANON ESTATE
1006 Monticello Road
Napa 94558
967-3520
Beaucanon_winery@msn.com

BEAULIEU VINEYARD
1960 St. Helena Highway
Rutherford 94573
967-5200
bvinfo@bvwines.com
www.bvwines.com

BELL WINE CELLARS
6200 Washington Street
Yountville 94599
944-1673
info@bellwine.com
www.bellwine.com

BENESSERE VINEYARDS
1010 Big Tree Road
St. Helena 94574
963-5853
www.benesserevineyards.com

BERINGER VINEYARDS
2000 Main Street
St. Helena 94574
963-7115
www.beringer.com

BETTINELLI VINEYARDS
7850 Silverado Trail
Oakville 94952
967-4141
info@bettinelli.com
www.bettinelli.com

BIGHORN CELLARS
3103 Silverado Trail
Napa 94558
224-6565
bighorn@bighorncellars.com
www.bighorncellars.com

BLOCKHEADIA WINERY
1764 Scott Street
St. Helena 94574
963-8593
info@blockheadia.com
www.blockheadia.com

BOUCHAINE VINEYARDS
1075 Buchli Station Road
Napa 94559
252-9065
info@bouchaine.com
www.bouchaine.com

BROOKDALE VINEYARDS
4006 Silverado Trail
Napa 94558
258-1454
mike@brookdalewine.com
www.brookdalewine.com

BUEHLER VINEYARDS
820 Greenfield Road
St. Helena 94574
963-2155
buehlers@pacbell.net
www.buehlervineyards.com

BURGESS CELLARS
1108 Deer Park Road
St. Helena 94574
963-4766
www.burgesscellars.com

CAFARO CELLARS
1591 Dean York Lane
St. Helena 94574
963-7181
cafaro@cafaro.com
www.cafaro.com

CAIN VINEYARD & WINERY
3800 Langtry Road
St. Helena 94574
963-1616
winery@cainfive.com
www.cainfive.com

CAKEBREAD CELLARS
8300 St. Helena Highway
Rutherford 94573
(800) 588-0298
cellars@cakebread.com
www.cakebread.com

CALAFIA CELLARS
1800 Mount Veeder Road
Napa 94558
253-9055

OLIVER CALDWELL CELLARS
3480 St. Helena Highway
St. Helena 94574
963-2037
info@caldwellcellars.com
www.caldwellcellars.com

CARDINALE ESTATE
7600 St. Helena Highway
Oakville 94562
948-2643
cardinale.info@cardinale.com
www.cardinale.com

CARNEROS CREEK WINERY
1285 Dealy Lane
Napa 94559
253-9463
wineinfo@carneroscreek.com
www.carneroscreek.com

CASA NUESTRA WINERY &
VINEYARDS
3451 Silverado Trail North
St. Helena 94574
963-5783
info@casanuestra.com
www.casanuestra.com

CATACULA LAKE WINERY
4105 Chiles Pope Valley Road
St. Helena 94574
965-1104
cataculalakewinery@yahoo.com
www.cataculalake.com

CAYMUS VINEYARDS
8700 Conn Creek Road
St. Helena 94573
963-4204
www.caymus.com

CEJA VINEYARDS
P.O. Box 5957
Napa 94581
(877) 633-3954 or 255-3954
wine@cejavineyards.com
www.cejavineyards.com

CHAPPELLET WINERY
1581 Sage Canyon Road
St. Helena 94574
963-7136
winery@chappellet.com
www.chappellet.com

CHATEAU BOSWELL
3468 Silverado Trail
St. Helena 94574
963-5472

CHATEAU CHEVRE WINERY
2030 Hoffman Lane
Yountville 94558
944-2184

CHATEAU MONTELENA
1429 Tubbs Lane
Calistoga 94515
942-5105
reservations@montelena.com
www.montelena.com

CHATEAU POTELLE
3875 Mount Veeder Road
Napa 94558
255-9440
info@chateaupotelle.com
www.chateaupotelle.com

CHATEAU WOLTNER
150 White Cottage Road South
Angwin 94508
965-2445

CHIMNEY ROCK WINERY
5350 Silverado Trail
Napa 94558
(800) 257-2641
club@chimneyrock.com
www.chimneyrock.com

CLARK-CLAUDON VINEYARDS
P.O. Box 15
St. Helena 94574
965-9393
wine@clarkclaudon.com
www.clarkclaudon.com

CLIFF LEDE VINEYARDS
1473 Yountville Cross Road
Yountville 94599
428-2259
www.cliffledevineyards.com

CLOS DU VAL
5330 Silverado Trail
Napa 94558
259-2225
cdv@closduval.com
www.closduval.com

CLOS PEGASE
1060 Dunaweal Lane
Calistoga 94515
942-4981
info@clospegase.com
www.clospegase.com

CONN CREEK WINERY
8711 Silverado Trail
St. Helena 94574
963-9100
info@conncreek.com
www.conncreek.com

CONSTANT-DIAMOND
MOUNTAIN VINEYARDS
2121 Diamond Mountain Road
Calistoga 94515
942-0707

CORISON WINERY
987 St. Helena Highway
St. Helena 94574
963-0826

COSENTINO WINERY
7415 St. Helena Highway
Yountville 94599
944-1220
finewines@cosentinowinery.com
www.cosentinowinery.com

COSTELLO VINEYARDS
1200 Orchard Avenue
Napa 94558
252-8483

ROBERT CRAIG WINE CELLARS
880 Vallejo Street
Napa 94559
252-2250, ext. 1
rachel@robertcraigwine.com
www.robertcraigwine.com

CRANE FAMILY VINEYARDS
1051 Borrette Lane
Napa 94558
259-1075
info@cranefamilyvineyards.com
www.cranefamilyvineyards.com

CRICHTON HALL VINEYARD
1150 Darms Lane
Napa 94558
224-4200
info@crichtonhall.com
www.crichtonhall.com

CUVAISON WINERY
4550 Silverado Trail
Calistoga 94515
942-6266
info@cuvaison.com
www.cuvaison.com

DALLA VALLE VINEYARDS
7776 Silverado Trail
Napa 94558
944-2676
www.dallavallevineyards.com

DARIOUSH
4240 Silverado Trail
Napa 94558
257-2345
info@darioush.com
www.darioush.com

DEER PARK WINERY
1000 Deer Park Road
Deer Park 94576
963-5411

DEL DOTTO VINEYARDS
1291 West Zinfandel Lane
St. Helena 94574
963-2134
mail@deldottovineyards.com
www.deldottovineyards.com

DIAMOND CREEK VINEYARDS
1500 Diamond Mountain Road
Calistoga 94515
942-6926
www.diamondcreekvineyards.com

DIAMOND OAKS WINERY
1595 Oakville Grade
Oakville 94562
948-3000
www.diamond-oaks.com

DOMAINE CARNEROS
1240 Duhig Road
Napa 94559
257-0101
www.domainecarneros.com

DOMAINE CHANDON
1 California Drive
Yountville 94599
944-2280
info@chandon.com
www.chandon.com

DOMAINE CHARBAY WINERY &
DISTILLERY
4001 Spring Mountain Road
St. Helena 94574
(800) 634-7845
info@charbay.com
www.charbay.com

DOMAINE MONTREAUX
4242 Big Ranch Road
Napa 94558
253-2802
wine@monticello-corleyfamily
vineyards.com

DOMINUS ESTATE
2570 Napanook Road
Yountville 94599
944-8954
dominus@napanet.net
www.dominusestate.com

DOWNING FAMILY VINEYARDS
7830 St. Helena Highway
Oakville 94562
399-9463
info@dfwines.com
www.dfwines.com

DUCKHORN VINEYARDS
1000 Lodi Lane
St. Helena 94574
(888) 354-8885
welcome@duckhorn.com
www.duckhorn.com

DUNN VINEYARDS
805 White Cottage Road North
Angwin 94508
965-3642

DUTCH HENRY WINERY
4310 Silverado Trail
Calistoga 94515
942-5771
info@dutchhenry.com
www.dutchhenry.com

DYER VINEYARD
1501 Diamond Mountain Road
Calistoga 94515
942-5502
www.dyerwine.com

EAGLE & ROSE ESTATE
1844 Pope Canyon Road
Pope Valley 94567
965-9463
info@eagleandrose.com
www.eagleandrose.com

EHLERS ESTATE
3222 Ehlers Lane
St. Helena 94574
963-5972
info@ehlersestate.com
www.ehlersestate.com

EHLERS GROVE/CARTLIDGE &
BROWNE WINERY
1142 Main Street
St. Helena 94574
967-1042
ehlers@ehlersgrove.com
www.ehlersgrove.com

ELAN VINEYARDS
4500 Atlas Peak Road
Napa 94558
252-3339
elanwine@aol.com
www.elanvineyards.com

ELKHORN PEAK CELLARS
200 Polson Road
Napa 94559
(800) 829-5082
epcellars@aol.com
www.elkhornpeak.com

EL MOLINO WINERY
P.O. Box 306
St. Helena 94574
963-3632
info@elmolinowinery.com
www.elmolinowinery.com

ELYSE WINERY
2100 Hoffman Lane
Yountville 94558
944-2900
info@elysewinery.com
www.elysewinery.com

ESQUISSE
1155 Mee Lane
St. Helena 94574
963-9999
www.esquissewines.com

ETUDE WINES
P.O. Box 3382
Napa 94558
257-5300
www.etudewines.com

HANS FAHDEN VINEYARDS
4855 Petrified Forest Road
Calistoga 94515
942-6760
www.hansfahden.com

FARELLA-PARK VINEYARDS
2222 North Third Avenue
Napa 94558
254-9489
fpvwines@aol.com

FAR NIENTE WINERY
1 Acacia Lane
Oakville 94562
944-2861
welcome@farniente.com
www.farniente.com

FIFE VINEYARDS
7830-40 St. Helena Highway
Oakville 94562
963-1534 or 485-0323
info@fifevineyards.com
www.fifevineyards.com

FLORA SPRINGS WINERY
677 St. Helena Highway
St. Helena 94574
967-8032
info@florasprings.com
www.florasprings.com

FOLIE À DEUX
3070 St. Helena Highway
St. Helena 94574
963-1160
tasting@folieadeux.com
www.folieadeux.com

FORMAN VINEYARD
1501 Big Rock Road
St. Helena 94574
963-3900
sales@formanvineyard.com

FRANCISCAN OAKVILLE ESTATE
1178 Galleron Road
St. Helena 94574
963-7111
www.franciscan.com

FRANK FAMILY VINEYARDS
1091 Larkmead Lane
Calistoga 94515
(800) 574-9463

FRANUS WINE COMPANY
2055 Hoffman Lane
Yountville 94599
945-0542
peter@franuswine.com
www.franuswine.com

FREEMARK ABBEY WINERY
3022 St. Helena Highway North
St. Helena 94574
963-9698
wineinfo@freemarkabbey.com
www.freemarkabbey.com

FRIAS FAMILY VINEYARD
3125 North St. Helena Highway
St. Helena 94574
(415) 566-2419
friasvineyard@aol.com
www.friasfamilyvineyard.com

FRISINGER CELLARS
2277 Dry Creek Road
Napa 94558
255-3749

FROG'S LEAP WINERY
8815 Conn Creek Road
Rutherford 94573
963-4704
ribbit@frogsleap.com
www.frogsleap.com

GARGIULO VINEYARDS
575 Oakville Crossroad
Napa 94558
944-2770
april@gargiulovineyards.com
www.gargiulovineyards.com

GIRARD WINERY
1241 Adams Street #1107
St. Helena 94574
968-9760
pat@girardwinery.com
www.girardwinery.com

GODSPEED VINEYARDS
3655 Mount Veeder Road
Napa 94558
254-7766
ksiwnapa@concentric.net

GOOSECROSS CELLARS
1119 State Lane
Yountville 94599
944-1986
hospitality@goosecross.com
www.goosecross.com

JOEL GOTT WINES
945 Main Street
St. Helena 94574
963-3365
info@gottwines.com
www.gottwines.com

GRACE FAMILY VINEYARDS
1210 Rockland Road
St. Helena 94574
963-0808
www.gracefamilyvineyards.com

GRAESER WINERY
255 Petrified Forest Road
Calistoga 94515
942-4437
richard@graeserwinery.com
www.graeserwinery.com

GREEN AND RED VINEYARD
3208 Chiles Valley Road
St. Helena 94574
965-2346
www.greenandred.com

GRGICH HILLS CELLAR
1829 St. Helena Highway
Rutherford 94573
(800) 532-3057
info@grgich.com
www.grgich.com

GROTH VINEYARDS & WINERY
750 Oakville Cross Road
Oakville 94562
944-0290
info@grothwines.com
www.grothwines.com

GUILLAMS VINEYARDS
3851 Spring Mountain Road
St. Helena 94574
963-9059
guillam@napanet.net

HAGAFEN CELLARS
4160 Silverado Trail
Napa 94558
252-0781
info@hagafen.com
www.hagafen.com

HALL NAPA VALLEY
401 S. St. Helena Highway
St. Helena 94574
967-2620
www.hallwines.com

HARLAN ESTATE
1551 Oakville Grade
Oakville 94562
944-1441
weaver@harlanestate.com
www.harlanestate.com

HARRISON VINEYARDS
1527 Sage Canyon Road
St. Helena 94574
963-8271
info@harrisonvineyards.com
www.harrisonvineyards.com

HARTWELL VINEYARDS
5795 Silverado Trail
Napa 94558
255-4269
info@hartwellvineyards.com
www.hartwellvineyards.com

HAVENS WINE CELLARS
2055 Hoffman Lane
Napa 94558
261-2000
info@havenswine.com
www.havenswine.com

HEITZ WINE CELLARS
436 St. Helena Highway South
St. Helena 94574
963-3542
www.heitzcellar.com

HELENA VIEW/JOHNSTON
VINEYARDS
3500 Highway 128
Calistoga 94515
942-4956
www.helenaview.com

THE HESS COLLECTION WINERY
4411 Redwood Road
Napa 94558
255-1144
info@hesscollection.com
www.hesscollection.com

WILLIAM HILL WINERY
1761 Atlas Peak Road
Napa 94558
224-4477
whw_info@williamhillwinery.com
www.williamhillwinery.com

HONIG VINEYARD & WINERY
850 Rutherford Road
Rutherford 94573
963-5618
info@honigwine.com
www.honigwine.com

HUMANITAS
1081 Round Hill Circle
Napa 94558
259-0349
info@humanitaswines.com
www.humanitaswines.com

JADE MOUNTAIN
2750 Las Amigas Road
Napa 94559
226-9997
www.chalonewinegroup.com

JARVIS WINERY
2970 Monticello Road
Napa 94559
255-5280
info@jarviswines.com
www.jarviswines.com

JESSUP CELLARS
3377 Solano Avenue, Suite 402
Napa 94558
224-7067
wine@jessupcellars.com
www.jessupcellars.com

JUDD'S HILL
P.O. Box 415
St. Helena 94574
963-9093
info@juddshill.com
www.juddshill.com

KATE'S VINEYARD
5211 Big Ranch Road
Napa 94558
255-2644
info@katesvineyard.com
www.katesvineyard.com

ROBERT KEENAN WINERY
3660 Spring Mountain Road
St. Helena 94574
963-9177
rkw@keenanwinery.com
www.keenanwinery.com

KELHAM VINEYARDS
360 Zinfandel Lane
St. Helena 94574
963-2000
info@kelhamvineyards.com
www.kelhamvineyards.com

KIRKLAND RANCH WINERY
1 Kirkland Ranch Road
Napa 94558
254-9100
info@kirklandranchwinery.com
www.kirklandranchwinery.com

KORNELL CHAMPAGNE CELLARS
1091 Larkmead Lane
Calistoga 94515
942-0859

KOVES-NEWLAN VINEYARDS &
WINERY
5225 Solano Avenue
Napa 94558
257-2399
sales@kovesnewlanwine.com
www.kovesnewlanwine.com

CHARLES KRUG WINERY
2800 Main Street
St. Helena 94574
800-682-5784
retail@pmondavi.com
www.charleskrug.com

LADERA VINEYARDS
150 White Cottage Road South
Angwin 94508
965-2445
info@laderavineyards.com
www.laderavineyards.com

LAIL VINEYARDS
320 Stoneridge Road
Angwin 94508
963-3329
www.lailvineyards.com

LAIRD FAMILY ESTATE
5055 Solano Avenue
Napa 94558
(887) 297-4902, ext. 26
generalinfo@lairdfamilyestate.com
www.lairdfamilyestate.com

LA JOTA VINEYARD
1102 Las Posadas Road
Angwin 94508
965-3020
info@lajotavineyardco.com
www.lajotavineyardco.com

LAMBORN FAMILY VINEYARDS
NAPA WINE COMPANY
120 Village Square #13
Orinda 94563
(925) 254-0511
www.lamborn.com

HERB LAMB VINEYARD
P.O. Box 225
St. Helena 94574
967-9752
info@herblambvineyard.com
www.herblambvineyard.com

LARKMEAD VINEYARDS
P.O. Box 309
St. Helena 94575
942-6605
info@larkmead.com
www.larkmead.com

LIPARITA CELLARS
410 La Fata Street #200
St. Helena 94574
963-2775
info@liparita.com
www.liparita.com

LIVINGSTON-MOFFETT WINERY
1895 Cabernet Lane
St. Helena 92574
963-2120
info@livingstonwines.com
www.livingstonwines.com

LOKOYA
7600 St. Helena Highway
Oakville 94562
944-2807
lokoya.info@lokoya.com
www.lokoya.com

LONG MEADOW RANCH
1775 Whitehall Lane
St. Helena 94574
963-4555
info@longmeadowranch.com
www.longmeadowranch.com

LONG VINEYARDS
1535 Sage Canyon Road
St. Helena 94574
963-2496
info@longvineyards.com
www.longvineyards.com

LUNA VINEYARDS
2921 Silverado Trail
Napa 94558
255-2474
lunatics@lunavineyards.com
www.lunavineyards.com

MADONNA ESTATE WINERY/
MONT ST. JOHN CELLARS
5400 Old Sonoma Road
Napa 94559
255-8864
mail@madonnaestate.com
www.madonnaestate.com

MADRIGAL VINEYARDS
Napa Wine Company
7840 St. Helena Highway
Oakville 94562
(800) 848-9630
retail@napawineco.com
www.napawineco.com

MARKHAM VINEYARDS
2812 St. Helena Highway North
St. Helena 94574
963-5292
admin@markhamvineyards.com
www.markhamvineyards.com

MARSTON FAMILY VINEYARD
3600 White Sulphur Springs Road
St. Helena 94574
963-8490
info@marstonfamilyvineyard.com
www.marstonfamilyvineyard.com

LOUIS M. MARTINI WINERY
254 St. Helena Highway South
St. Helena 94574
963-2736
info@louismartini.com
www.louismartini.com

MAYACAMAS VINEYARDS
1155 Lokoya Road
Napa 94558
224-4030
mayacama@napanet.net
www.mayacamas.com

MCKENZIE-MUELLER VINEYARDS
2350 Las Amigas Road
Napa 94559
252-0186
www.mckenziemueller.com

MENDELSON VINEYARD
1226 Third Street
Napa 94559
255-7825
Richard@mendelsonwines.com
www.mendelsonvineyard.com

MERRYVALE VINEYARDS
1000 Main Street
St. Helena 94574
963-7777
www.merryvale.com

PETER MICHAEL WINERY
12400 Ida Clayton Road
Calistoga 94515
942-4459
wineclub@petermichaelwinery.com
www.petermichaelwinery.com

MILAT VINEYARDS
1091 St. Helena Highway South
St. Helena 94574
(800) 546-4528
info@milat.com
www.milat.com

MINER FAMILY VINEYARDS
7850 Silverado Trail
Oakville 94562
944-9500
info@minerwines.com
www.minerwines.com

ROBERT MONDAVI WINERY
7801 St. Helena Highway South
Oakville 94562
(888) 766-6328
info@robertmondavi.com
www.robertmondavi.com

MONTICELLO VINEYARDS
4242 Big Ranch Road
Napa 94558
253-2802
wine@CorleyFamilyNapaValley.com
www.CorleyFamilyNapaValley.com

MOSS CREEK WINERY
6015 Steele Canyon Road
Napa 94558
252-1295

MOUNT VEEDER WINERY
1999 Mount Veeder Road
Napa 94558
(800) 529-9463
www.mtveeder.com

MUMM NAPA ESTATES
8445 Silverado Trail
Rutherford 94573
967-7700
mumm_info@mummcuveenapa.com
www.mummcuveenapa.com

NAPA CELLARS
7481 St. Helena Highway
Oakville 94562
944-2565
hollya@napacellars.com
www.napacellars.com

NAPA WINE COMPANY
7830 St. Helena Highway
Oakville 94562
944-1710
retail@napawineco.com
www.napawineco.com

NEAL FAMILY VINEYARDS
716 Liparita Road
Angwin 94508
965-2800
info@nealvineyards.com
www.nealvineyards.com

NEWTON VINEYARD
2555 Madrona Avenue
St. Helena 94574
963-9000

NEYERS VINEYARD
P.O. Box 1028
St. Helena 94574
963-8840

NICHELINI WINERY
2950 Sage Canyon Road
St. Helena 94574
963-0717
www.nicheliniwinery.com

NICKEL & NICKEL
8164 St. Helena Highway
Oakville 94562
944-0693
info@nickelandnickel.com
www.nickelandnickel.com

NIEBAUM-COPPOLA ESTATE
WINERY
1991 St. Helena Highway
Rutherford 94573
968-1100
info@niebaum-coppola.com
www.niebaum-coppola.com

OAKFORD VINEYARDS
1575 Oakville Grade Road
Oakville 94562
945-0445
info@oakfordvineyards.com
www.oakfordvineyards.com

OAKVILLE RANCH VINEYARDS
7850 Silverado Trail
Oakville 94562
944-9500
info@minerwines.com
www.minerwines.com

OPUS ONE
7900 St. Helena Highway
Oakville 94562
944-9442
info@opusonewinery.com
www.opusonewinery.com

ORIGIN-NAPA
P.O. Box 670
St. Helena 94574
968-9111
customerservice@originnapa.com
www.originnapa.com

PAHLMEYER WINERY
P.O. Box 2410
Napa 94558
255-2321
info@pahlmeyer.com
www.pahlmeyer.com

PAOLETTI ESTATES WINERY
4501 Silverado Trail
Calistoga 94515
942-0689
gianni@giannipaoletti.com
www.giannipaoletti.com

PARADIGM WINERY
P.O. Box 323
Oakville 94562
944-1683
info@paradigmwinery.com
www.paradigmwinery.com

PARADUXX
1000 Lodi Lane
St. Helena 94574
963-7595
welcome@duckhorn.com
www.duckhorn.com

ROBERT PECOTA WINERY
3299 Bennett Lane
Calistoga 94515
942-6625
info@robertpecotawinery.com
www.robertpecotawinery.com

PEJU PROVINCE
8466 St. Helena Highway
Rutherford 94573
963-3600
contactus@peju.com
www.peju.com

MARIO-PERELLI–MINETTI WINERY
& WILLIAM HARRISON WINERY
1443 Silverado Trail
St. Helena 94574
963-8310

JOSEPH PHELPS VINEYARDS
200 Taplin Road
St. Helena 94574
963-2745
jpvwines@aol.com
www.jpvwines.com

PINA CELLARS
8060 Silverado Trail
Rutherford 94573
944-2229

PINE RIDGE WINERY
5901 Silverado Trail
Napa 94558
(800) 575-9777
info@pineridgewine.com
www.pineridgewinery.com

PLUMPJACK WINERY
620 Oakville Cross Road
Oakville 94562
945-1220
winery@plumpjack.com
www.plumpjack.com

POPE VALLEY WINERY
6613 Pope Valley Road
Pope Valley 94567
965-1246
info@popevalleywinery.com
www.popevalleywinery.com

PRAGER WINERY AND
PORT WORKS
1281 Lewelling Lane
St. Helena 94574
963-7678
ahport@pragerport.com
www.pragerport.com

PRIDE MOUNTAIN VINEYARDS
4026 Spring Mountain Road
St. Helena 94574
963-4949
contactus@pridewines.com
www.pridewines.com

PROVENANCE VINEYARDS
P.O. Box 668
Rutherford 94573
968-3633
info@provenancevineyards.com
www.provenancevineyards.com

QUINTESSA
1601 Silverado Trail
Rutherford 94573
967-1601
www.quintessa.com

QUIXOTE WINERY
6126 Silverado Trail
Napa 94558
944-2659

KENT RASMUSSEN WINERY
1001 Silverado Trail
St. Helena 94574
963-5667
info@kentrasmussenwinery.com
www.ramsaywines.com

RAYMOND VINEYARD & CELLAR
849 Zinfandel Lane
St. Helena 94574
963-3141
director@raymondwine.com
www.raymondwine.com

REGUSCI WINERY
5584 Silverado Trail
Napa 94558
254-0403
info@regusciwinery.com
www.regusciwinery.com

RENTERIA
6236 Silverado Trail
Napa 94558
944-1382
www.renteriawines.com

REVERIE ON DIAMOND
MOUNTAIN
1520 Diamond Mountain Road
Calistoga 94515
942-6800
email@reveriewine.com
www.reveriewine.com

REYNOLDS FAMILY WINERY
3266 Silverado Trail
Napa 94558
258-2558
info@reynoldsfamilywinery.com
www.reynoldsfamilywinery.com

RISTOW ESTATE
5040 Silverado Trail
Napa 94558
252-8379
email@ristowestate.com
www.ristowestate.com

RITCHIE CREEK VINEYARD
4024 Spring Mountain Road
St. Helena 94574
963-4661
rcv@napanet.net
www.ritchiecreek.com

RIVERA VINEYARDS
3225 Soda Canyon Road
Napa 94559
254-7393
www.riveravineyards.com

ROMBAUER VINEYARDS
3522 Silverado Trail
St. Helena 94574
963-5170
sheana@rombauervineyards.com
www.rombauervineyards.com

ROUND HILL VINEYARDS &
CELLARS
1680 Silverado Trail
St. Helena 94574
968-3200
sales@roundhillwines.com
www.roundhillwines.com

RUDD
500 Oakville Cross Road
Oakville 94562
944-8577

RUSTRIDGE WINERY
2910 Lower Chiles Valley Road
St. Helena 94574
965-9353
rustridg@napanet.net
www.rustridge.com

RUTHERFORD GROVE WINERY
1673 St. Helena Highway
Rutherford 94573
963-0544
info@rutherfordgrove.com
www.rutherfordgrove.com

RUTHERFORD HILL WINERY
200 Rutherford Hill Road
Rutherford 94573
963-1871
info@rutherfordhill.com
www.rutherfordhill.com

RUTHERFORD RANCH
VINEYARDS
1680 Silverado Trail
St. Helena 94574
968-3200
www.rutherfordranch.com

SADDLEBACK CELLARS
7802 Money Road
Oakville 94562
944-1305
www.saddlebackcellars.com

ST. CLEMENT VINEYARDS
2867 St. Helena Highway North
St. Helena 94574
967-3033 or (800) 331-8266
info@stclement.com
www.stclement.com

ST. SUPÉRY VINEYARDS
AND WINERY
8440 St. Helena Highway
Rutherford 94573
963-4507 or (800) 942-0809
divinecab@stsupery.com
www.stsupery.com

SAINTSBURY
1500 Los Carneros Avenue
Napa 94559
252-0592
info@saintsbury.com
www.saintsbury.com

SALVESTRIN ESTATE VINEYARD
& WINERY
397 Main Street
St. Helena 94574
963-5105
shannon@salvestrinwinery.com
www.salvestrinwinery.com

SAVIEZ VINEYARDS
4060 Silverado Trail North
Calistoga 94515
942-5889
info@saviezvineyards.com
www.saviezvineyards.com

SAWYER CELLARS
8350 St. Helena Highway
Rutherford 94573
963-1980
www.sawyercellars.com

SCHRAMSBERG VINEYARDS
1400 Schramsberg Road
Calistoga 94515
942-4558
info@schramsberg.com
www.schramsberg.com

SCHUETZ OLES WINERY
P.O. Box 834
St. Helena 94574
963-5121
rischuetz@earthlink.net
www.schuetzoles.com

SCHWEIGER VINEYARDS
4015 Spring Mountain Road
St. Helena 94574
963-4882
svwine@schweigervineyards.com
www.schweigervineyards.com

SCREAMING EAGLE
P.O. Box 134
Oakville 94562
944-0749
www.screamingeagle.com

SEAVEY VINEYARD
1310 Conn Valley Road
St. Helena 94574
963-8339
info@seaveyvineyard.com
www.seaveyvineyard.com

SELENE WINES
P.O. Box 3131
Napa 94458
258-8119
mia@selenewines.com
www.selenewines.com

SEQUOIA GROVE VINEYARDS
8338 St. Helena Highway
Napa 94558
944-2945
info@sequoiagrove.com
www.sequoiagrove.com

SHAFER VINEYARDS
6154 Silverado Trail
Napa 94558
944-2877
info@shafervineyards.com
www.shafervineyards.com

SHERWIN FAMILY VINEYARDS
4060 Spring Mountain Road
St. Helena 94574
963-1154
www.sherwinfamilyvineyards.com

SHOWKET VINEYARDS
P.O. Box 350
Oakville 94562
944-1101
dks@showketvineyards.com
www.showketvineyards.com

SHYPOKE CELLARS
4170 St. Helena Highway North
Calistoga 94515
942-0420

SIGNORELLO VINEYARDS
4500 Silverado Trail
Napa 94558
255-5990
info@signorellovineyards.com
www.signorellovineyards.com

SILVERADO HILL CELLARS
3105 Silverado Trail
Napa 94558
253-9306

SILVERADO VINEYARDS
6121 Silverado Trail
Napa 94558
257-1770
info@silveradovineyards.com
www.silveradovineyards.com

SILVER OAK CELLARS
915 Oakville Cross Road
Oakville 94562
944-8808
info@silveroak.com
www.silveroak.com

SILVER ROSE CELLARS
400 Silverado Trail
Calistoga 94515
942-9581
silvrose@napanet.net
www.silverrose.com

ROBERT SINSKEY VINEYARDS
6320 Silverado Trail
Napa 94558
944-9090
info@robertsinskey.com
www.robertsinskey.com

SKY VINEYARDS
1500 Lokoya Drive
Napa 94558
935-1391
info@skyvineyards.com
www.skyvineyards.com

SMITH-MARDRONE VINEYARDS
& WINERY
4022 Spring Mountain Road
St. Helena 94574
963-2283
info@smithmadrone.com
www.smithmadrone.com

SPARROW LANE VINEYARDS
1455 Summit Lake Drive
Angwin 94508
965-9130
www.sparrowlane.com

SPELLETICH CELLARS
195 Edgewood Lane
Angwin 94508
965-0952
wines@spellwine.com
www.spellwines.com

SPOTTSWOODE WINERY
1902 Madrona Avenue
St. Helena 94574
963-0134
spottswd@fcs.net
www.spottswoode.com

SPRING MOUNTAIN VINEYARD
P.O. Box 991
St. Helena 94574
967-4188
www.springmtn.com

STAGLIN FAMILY VINEYARD
P.O. Box 680
Rutherford 94573
944-0477
info@staglinfamily.com
www.staglinfamily.com

STAG'S LEAP WINE CELLARS
5766 Silverado Trail
Napa 94558
944-2020
retail@cask23.com
www.stagsleapwinecellars.com

STAGS' LEAP WINERY
6150 Silverado Trail
Napa 94558
944-1303
www.stagsleap.com

STAR HILL WINERY
1075 Shadybrook Lane
Napa 94558
255-1957
winestar@aol.com
www.starhill.com

STELTZNER VINEYARDS
5998 Silverado Trail
Napa 94558
252-7272
wines@steltzner.com
www.steltzner.com

D. R. STEPHENS ESTATE
1860 Howell Mountain Road
St. Helena 94574
781-8000
info@drstephenswines.com
www.drstephenswines.com

STERLING VINEYARDS
1111 Dunaweal Lane
Calistoga 94515
942-3344
concierge@svclub.com
www.sterlingvineyards.com

STONEGATE WINERY
1183 Dunaweal Lane
Calistoga 94515
942-6500
info@stonegatewinery.com
www.stonegatewinery.com

STONEY SPRINGS WINERY
264 Crystal Springs Road
St. Helena 94574
963-7760

STONY HILL VINEYARD
P.O. Box 308
St. Helena 94574
963-2636
www.stonyhillvineyard.com

STORYBOOK MOUNTAIN
VINEYARDS
3835 Highway 128
Calistoga 94515
942-5310
sigstory@storybookwines.com
www.storybookwines.com

STRAUS VINEYARDS
315 Franz Valley School Road
Calistoga 94515
942-1238

SULLIVAN VINEYARDS
1090 Galleron Road
Rutherford 94573
(877) 244-7337
www.sullivanwine.com

SUMMERS WINERY
1171 Tubbs Lane
Calistoga 94515
942-5508
swmarketing@direcway.com
www.summerswinery.com

SUMMIT LAKE VINEYARDS
AND WINERY
2000 Summit Lake Road
Angwin 94500
965-2488
summitlake@summitlakevineyards.com
www.summitlakevineyards.com

SUTTER HOME WINERY/
TRINCHERO FAMILY ESTATES
277 St. Helena Highway South
St. Helena 94574
963-3104, ext. 4208
info@sutterhome.com
www.sutterhome.com

SWANSON VINEYARDS
AND WINERY
1271 Manley Lane
Rutherford 94573
967-3500
www.swansonvineyards.com

THE TERRACES
1450 Silverado Trail
St. Helena 94574
963-1707
timm@terraceswine.com
www.terraceswine.com

TERRA VALENTINE
3787 Spring Mountain Road
St. Helena 94574
967-8340
info@terravalentine.com
www.terravalentine.com

GUSTAVO THRACE WINERY
1146 First Street
Napa 94559
257-6796
gustavot@napanet.net
www.gustavothrace.com

PHILIP TOGNI VINEYARD
3780 Spring Mountain Road
St. Helena 94574
963-3731

TREFETHEN VINEYARDS
1160 Oak Knoll Avenue
Napa 94558
255-7700
winery@trefethen.com
www.trefethen.com

TRES SABORES
1620 South Whitehall Lane
St. Helena 94574
967-8027
www.tressabores.com

TRINCHERO FAMILY ESTATES
277 St. Helena Highway South
St. Helena 94574
963-3104
www.trincherowinery.com

TRUCHARD VINEYARDS
3234 Old Sonoma Road
Napa 94559
253-7153
www.truchardvineyards.com

TUDAL WINERY
1015 Big Tree Road
St. Helena 94574
963-3947

TULOCAY WINERY
1426 Coombsville Road
Napa 94558
255-4064
http://tulocay.com

TURLEY WINE CELLARS
3358 St. Helena Highway
St. Helena 94574
963-0940
www.turleywinecellars.com

TURNBULL WINE CELLARS
8210 St. Helena Highway
Oakville 94562
963-5839
www.turnbullwines.com

TWOMEY CELLARS
1183 Dunaweal Lane
Calistoga 94515
942-7424 or (800) 505-4850
www.twomeycellars.com

V. SATTUI WINERY
1111 White Lane
St. Helena 94574
963-7774
info@vsattui.com
www.vsattui.com

VAN DER HEYDEN VINEYARDS
4057 Silverado Trail
Napa 94558
257-0130
vvwines@napanet.net
www.vanderheydenvineyards.com

VIADER VINEYARDS & WINERY
1120 Deer Park Road
Deer Park 94576
963-3816
www.viader.com

VIGIL VINEYARD WINES
3340 Highway 128
Calistoga 94515
537-3700
vigilwine@aol.com

VILLA ANDRIANA
1171 Tubbs Lane
Calistoga 94515
942-5508
swmarketing@direcway.com
www.summerswinery.com

VILLA HELENA WINERY
1455 Inglewood Avenue
St. Helena 94574
963-4334
vintner@pobox.com
www.geocities.com/villahelena

VILLA MT. EDEN
8711 Silverado Trail
St. Helena 94574
963-9100
info@villamteden.com
www.villamteden.com

VINE CLIFF WINERY
7400 Silverado Trail
Napa 94558
944-1364
info@vinecliff.com
www.vinecliff.com

VINEYARD 29
2929 Highway 29 North
St. Helena 94574
963-9292
www.vineyard29.com

VINOCE VINEYARDS
1245 Main Street
Napa 94558
944-8717
info@vinoce.com
www.vinoce.com

VOLKER EISELE FAMILY ESTATE
3080 Lower Chiles Valley Road
St. Helena 94574
965-2260
www.volkereiselevineyard.com
info@volkereiselevineyard.com

VON STRASSER WINERY
1510 Diamond Mountain Road
Calistoga 94515
942-0930
winemaker@vonstrasser.com
www.vonstrasser.com

W WINERY
3268 Villa Lane
Napa 94558
259-2811

WERMUTH WINERY
3942 Silverado Trail
Calistoga 94515
942-5924

WHITEHALL LANE WINERY
1563 St. Helena Highway
St. Helena 94574
(800) 963-9454
greatwine@whitehalllane.com
www.whitehalllane.com

WHITE ROCK VINEYARDS
1115 Loma Vista Drive
Napa 94558
257-7922
info@whiterockvineyards.com
www.whiterockvineyards.com

WHITFORD CELLARS
4047 East Third Avenue
Napa 94558
942-0840

WOLF FAMILY VINEYARDS
2125 Inglewood Avenue
St. Helena 94574
963-6042

X WINERY
PO Box 528
St. Helena 94574
968-0712
info@xwinery.com
www.xwinery.com

ZAHTILA VINEYARDS
2250 Lake County Highway
Calistoga 94515
942-9251
sales@zahtilavineyards.com
www.zahtilavineyards.com

ZD WINES
8383 Silverado Trail
Napa 94558
963-5188
info@zdwines.com
www.zdwines.com

INDEX

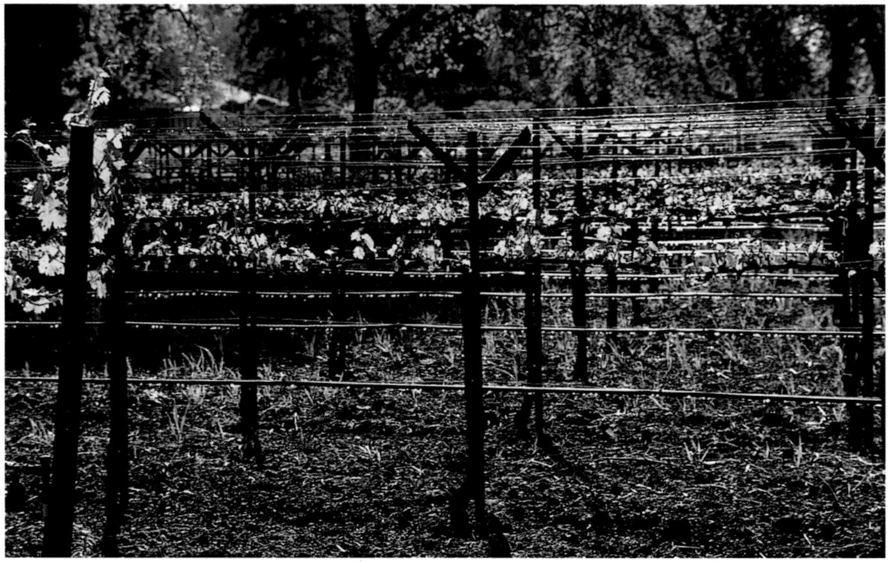